Prime Sport

Prime Sport

Triumph of the Athlete Mind

Jim Taylor, Ph.D.

Writers Club Press
New York San Jose Lincoln Shanghai

Prime Sport
Triumph of the Athlete Mind

Writers Club Press
an imprint of iUniverse.com, Inc.

. For information address:
iUniverse.com, Inc.
5220 S 16th, Ste. 200
Lincoln, NE 68512
www.iuniverse.com

Cover design by Gerald Sindell and Jim Taylor, Ph.D.

ISBN: 0-595-12651-0

Printed in the United States of America

ALSO BY DR. JIM TAYLOR

Prime Tennis
Prime Golf
Prime Ski Racing
The Mental Edge for Skiing
Psychology of Dance
Psychological Approaches to Sports Injury Rehabilitation
Comprehensive Sports Injury Management

**To order books by Dr. Jim Taylor or
for information about consultation and workshops contact:**

Jim Taylor, Ph.D.
Alpine/Taylor Consulting
P.O. Box 475313 San Francisco, CA 94147
tel: 415.345.9820 fax: 415.345.9830
e-mail: jtphd@alpinetaylor.com
web site: www.alpinetaylor.com

CONTENTS

PREFACE

When you compete in your sport, you will, in fact, be competing in two games. The obvious game is the competitive one that occurs against your opponent. The more important game, though, is the mental game that you will play inside your head against yourself. Here is a simple reality: If you don't win the mental game, you won't win the competitive game.

Contrary to what many athletes may think, at whatever level in which they're competing, the technical and physical aspects of their sport don't usually determine the winner. Athletes who compete at the same level are very similar technically and physically. For example, is Tiger Woods better technically than David Duval? Is Mark McGwire in better physical condition than Sammy Sosa? In both cases, the answer is clearly no. This is probably true for you and your biggest competitor as well. So, on any given day, what separates Lindsay Davenport from Martina Hingis, Drew Bledsoe from Brett Favre, or you from your opponent? The answer lies in who wins the mental game. Athletes who are the most motivated to perform their best, who have the greatest confidence in themselves, who perform best under pressure, who stay focused on their game, and who keep their emotions under control will most often emerge victorious.

Whenever I talk to serious athletes, I ask them what aspect of their sport seems to have the greatest impact on how they perform. Almost unanimously they say the mental part of their sport. I then ask how much time they put into their mental preparation. Their answer is almost always, little or no time.

Despite its obvious importance, the mental side of sport is most often neglected, at least until a problem arises. The mistake athletes make is that they don't treat their mental game the way they treat the physical and technical aspects of their sport. They don't wait to get injured before they do physical conditioning. They don't develop a technical flaw before they work on their technique. Rather, they do physical and technical training to prevent problems from arising. Athletes should approach the mental game in the same way.

Prime Sport was created to assist you in just this process, ensuring that mentally you are your best ally rather than your worst enemy. *Prime Sport* focuses on the essentials of the mental game and shows you how to make your mind work for you instead of against you.

Prime Sport is not magic dust and will not produce miracles. You would not expect increases in strength by lifting weights a few times or an improvement in technique by working on it for a few hours. The only way to improve any area, whether physical, technical, or mental, is through commitment, hard work, and patience.

Prime Sport describes issues and problems that are common to athletes regardless of their ability or experience, and are most likely also important to you. The information, techniques, and exercises in *Prime Sport* are designed to be "user-friendly;" easy to understand and apply directly to your sport. My goal is for you to read *Prime Sport* and go out tomorrow and use it immediately to improve your sports performance.

The information and strategies described in *Prime Sport* are not really sport skills or even sport psychology skills. Rather, they are life skills that can be used to enhance any part of your life. *Prime Sport* can be used in your sport or any area you choose to improve your performance and achieve your goals.

Prime Sport has several goals. First, to provide clear and understandable information about winning the mental game of sport. Second, to offer simple and practical techniques that you can easily use to raise your performances to a new level. Finally, to enable you to perform your best in your sport consistently.

> *"The biggest victories come over yourself, when you control your mind and your destiny."*
>
> **Hall of Fame baseball player Orlando Cepeda**

PRIME SPORT FOR ALL SPORTS

Prime Sport is written to benefit to athletes at all levels of ability and in every sport. Whether you are a novice or a professional, or compete in individual or team sports, the information and tools provided by *Prime Sport* can be applied to any sport setting.

A goal of writing *Prime Sport* has been to use a language that all athletes can relate to and can easily translate into the specific vocabulary of their sport. A difficulty with this process is that sports do not always share a common language. For example, athletes in some sports such as football, baseball, and tennis "play" their sport, while others such as figure skating, gymnastics, and track and field "perform" in their sport. Similarly, some sports, such as soccer and golf, compete in "games," while other sports, such as swimming and cycling, compete in "races," "meets," or "events."

To simplify communicating my ideas in *Prime Sport* (and to be fair to all sports), I will maintain a consistency of language by using "perform" and "competition" to describe athletes' participating in their sport. For athletes who do not participate those types of sports, I ask that you simply think of those words that are most appropriate for your sport.

USING PRIME SPORT

There's a great deal of information in *Prime Sport*. You shouldn't expect to take in and use all of the information the first time you read this book. Winning the mental game is a process that will parallel your own athletic development. It takes time to develop your physical and technical abilities. It will also take time to win the mental game.

Prime Sport has been specifically designed to make it easy for you to understand and use its information and techniques. It is organized around what I believe to be the most important mental issues that impact athletic performance. This structure enables you to select the areas most relevant to your sport. It allows you to find out exactly what you need to know for where you are in your sports participation and development. *Prime Sport* describes in detail the skills you need to develop for the mental areas that are most important to you. It shows you the exercises you need to practice to win the mental game.

I would suggest the following process in using *Prime Sport* to its greatest benefit. First, read the book all of the way through. As you read, make note of specific topics that are currently important to you. After reading the entire book, identify the issues that are most important to you and re-read those sections to better familiarize yourself with them. Then, select two or three areas on which you want to work. Experiment with different techniques to develop the areas you've chosen and select the ones you like best. Finally, implement those techniques in your daily schedule.

Now let's begin the exciting journey that culminates in the "triumph of the athlete mind."

> *"It's hard to separate the mental and physical. So much of what you do physically happens because you've thought about it and mentally prepared for it."*
>
> **Former NFL quarterback Dan Fouts**

ACKNOWLEDGEMENTS

Special thanks to Gerald Sindell, my manager, mentor, and friend. His creative and critical input to this book has been essential, and his support, vision, and perspective in my career and life have been invaluable.

I would like to thank the thousands of athletes and coaches with whom I have worked over the past 15 years. They have been my teachers.

Finally, I would like to express my love and appreciation to my parents, Ceci and Shel Taylor, for instilling in me a passion for maximizing human performance, which has become the focal point of my life's work.

SECTION I

INTRODUCTION

To begin *Prime Sport*, I would like to introduce you to several key concepts that will act as the foundation for the remainder of this book. One of the most popular phrases used in sport psychology is *peak performance*, which is typically defined as the highest level of performance an athlete can achieve, and it's considered to be the goal toward which all athletes should strive. When I came out of graduate school, peak performance was what I wanted the athletes with whom I worked to achieve.

But as I became more experienced as a psychologist and as a writer, I began to appreciate the power of words and how important it is that the words I use are highly descriptive of what I want to communicate. I decided that peak performance was not descriptive of what I wanted to convey to the athletes with whom I worked. I saw several problems with peak performance. One difficulty is that athletes can only maintain a peak for a very short time. Would you be satisfied if you performed well in one competition and then did poorly in subsequent ones? Also, once that peak is reached, there is only one way to go, and that is down. And with most peaks, the drop is steep and fast.

So I needed to find a phrase that accurately described what I wanted athletes to achieve. I struggled for several years unable to find such a phrase until one day a meeting of luck and readiness occurred. Walking through the meat section of a grocery store I saw a piece of beef with a sticker that read Prime Cut. I had an "aha" experience. I knew I was on to something. I returned to my office and looked up "prime" in the dictionary.

It was defined as "of the highest quality or value." I had finally found the phrase, "Prime Performance," which I believed was highly descriptive of what I wanted athletes to achieve.

I defined Prime Performance, or in this case, Prime Sport, as "performing at a consistently high level under the most challenging conditions." There are two essential words in this definition. The first key word is, "consistently." I'm not interested if an athlete can have only one or two great performances. That is not enough to be truly successful. I want athletes to be able to perform at a high level day in and day out, week in and week out, month in and month out. This doesn't mean performing perfectly. Rather, it means performing at a high level with only minimal ups and downs instead of the large swings in performance that are so common among athletes. The second key word is, "challenging." I'm not impressed if an athlete can perform well under ideal conditions against an easy opponent when they are well-rested and on top of their game. Anyone can do that. What makes the great athletes successful is their ability to perform their best under the worst possible conditions against a tough opponent when they're not on their game. If the athletes with whom I worked could attain this level of performance, Prime Sport, they would be successful.

A question you may ask is, Where does Prime Sport come from? Though I'll be focusing on its mental contributors, the mind is only one necessary part of Prime Sport. You must also be at a high level of physical health including being well-conditioned, well-rested, eating a balanced diet, and free from injury and illness. Prime Sport is also not possible if you're not technically sound. Your technical skills must be well-learned and your tactics must be ingrained. If you're physically, technically, tactically, and mentally prepared, then you will have the ability to achieve Prime Sport.

Now here is a question for you: Have you ever experienced Prime Sport? Do you know what it feels like to perform at that level? Let me describe some of the common experiences of Prime Sport. First, Prime Sport is effortless. It's comfortable, easy, and natural. You don't seem to have to try to do anything. Prime Sport is also automatic. There's little thought. The body does what it knows how to do and there's no mental interference getting in the way. You also experience sharpened senses. You see, hear, and feel everything more acutely than normal. I've heard Ken Griffey Jr. say that when he is swinging the bat well, the ball looks like the size of a grapefruit. At those times, he is experiencing Prime Sport. Also, time seems to slow down, enabling you to react more quickly. Prime Sport also has effortless focus. You're totally absorbed in the experience and are focused entirely on the process. You have no distractions or unnecessary thoughts that interfere with your performance. You have boundless energy. Your endurance seems endless and fatigue is simply not an issue. Finally, you experience what I call prime integration. Everything is working together. The physical, technical, tactical, and mental aspects of your sport are integrated into one path to Prime Sport.

> *"I channeled my mental, physical and emotional energies into my game."*
>
> **Chris Evert**

PHILOSOPHY OF PRIME SPORT

Before you can begin the process of developing Prime Sport, you need to create a foundation of beliefs about your sport on which you can build your mental skills. This foundation involves your attitude in three areas. First, your perspective on competition; what you think of it, how you feel about it, and how you approach it. Second, your view of yourself as a competitor; do you perform better in practice, competitions, or in pressure situations? Third, your attitude toward winning and losing; how you define winning and losing, and whether you know the essential roles that both winning and losing play in becoming the best athlete you can be. Clarifying your views in these three areas will make it easier to win the mental game and to achieve Prime Sport.

PRIME SPORT PERSPECTIVE ON COMPETITION

Sports are obviously important to you. You put a great deal of effort in your sports participation. Because of this, you put your ego on the line every time you perform. When you don't perform well, you're disappointed. This may not feel good, but it's natural because it means you care about your sport.

There is, however, a point at which athletes can lose perspective and their feelings toward their sport can hurt their performances. The key warning signal of this overinvolvement is "too." When they care *too* much, when it is *too* important to them, when they try *too* hard to win, when they press *too* much in critical competitive situations, then they have lost perspective.

In this "too" situation, athletes' investment in their sport is so great that it is no longer enjoyable. If you find yourself feeling this way, you should reevaluate what your sports participation means to you and how it impacts your life and your happiness. You will probably find that it plays too big a role in how you feel about yourself. When this happens, you not only perform poorly and lose more often, but you may find that your sport is no longer fun to you.

To perform your best and to have fun, you need to keep your sports participation in perspective. It may be important to you, but it should not be life or death. What is important is that you have a balanced view of your sport. Remember why you participate; it's fun, you like the exercise, it's a great way to socialize, it feels great to master a sport, and, yes, you like to compete and win. The Prime Sport view of competition means keeping your sport in perspective. If you have fun, work hard, enjoy the process of your sport, and do not care too much about winning and losing, you will enjoy the competition more, you will perform better, and you will win more often as well

"I have never made sports bigger than life. I just played and enjoyed them. My whole approach was based on what I could learn from sports."

NFL quarterback Rick Mirer

UPS AND DOWNS OF SPORT

Another aspect of the Prime Sport perspective on competition is recognizing and accepting the ups and downs of sport. In the history of sport, very few athletes have had perfect or near-perfect seasons: Wayne Gretzky, Steffi Graf, Michael Jordan, Nancy Lopez, Pedro Martinez. Even the best athletes have ups and downs. Since they do, then you should expect to have them too. It's not whether you have ups and downs in your sport, but how big the ups and downs are and how you respond to them. In fact, *Prime Sport* is devoted to assisting you in minimizing the ups and downs of sport.

In a down period, it's easy to get frustrated, angry, and depressed. You can feel really disappointed in how you're performing and can feel helpless to change it. You may want to just give up. But none of these feelings will help you accomplish your important goals: getting out of the down period and returning to a high level of performance. This is a skill that separates the great athletes from the good ones. The best athletes know how to get back to an up period quickly.

How do they do this? First, they keep the down period in perspective, knowing that it's a natural and expected part of sports. This attitude takes the pressure off them to rush back to a higher level of performance and keeps them from getting too upset. It also enables them to stay positive and motivated. Most importantly, they never give up. They keep working hard, no matter how bad it gets. These athletes look for the cause of their slump and then find a solution. If you maintain this attitude toward the ups and downs of sport, your down periods won't last as long and you'll more quickly swing back to an up period.

> *"If it weren't for the dark days, we wouldn't know what it is to walk in the light."*
>
> **NFL Hall of Fame player Earl Campbell**

SPORT IS ABOUT LOVE AND FUN

It's easy to lose sight of why you compete in sports. There are the trophies, rankings, and attention. Yet, when you get focused on the external benefits of sport, you may lose sight of the internal reasons why you compete. You may not have as much fun and you won't perform as well either. When this happens, you need to remind yourself of what sport is all about. Sports participation is about two things. First, it is about love: love of the sport, love of others, and love of yourself. If you love your sport, you have a chance to achieve Prime Sport.

Second, sports are about fun. Working hard, improving your performance, the joy of competition, and enjoying the process, win or lose, should all be fun. If you always remember that sports are about love and fun, then you will enjoy participating and you will perform your best.

> *"The most important thing is to love your sport. Never do it to please someone else—it has to be yours. That is all that will justify the hard work needed to achieve success."*
>
> **1968 Olympic figure skating champion Peggy Fleming**

PRIME SPORT FOR WINNING AND LOSING

Related to your attitude toward competition is your approach to winning and losing. How you define winning and losing, and your perceptions of the roles that winning and losing play in developing Prime Sport, will determine your ability to perform your best consistently.

Too often, winning and losing are defined narrowly with only one winner and many losers. The athlete who wins the competition is the winner and everyone else is a loser. But how many times have you performed well, yet lost. The fact is you can't usually control whether you win or lose. What you can control is the effort you put in and how well you perform. It's fruitless to strive for something that's out of your control, so winning and losing should be defined in terms of things over which you have control. With this in mind, I define winning as giving your best effort and performing to the best of your ability. I define losing as not trying your hardest and not performing as well as you can. The nice thing about this definition is that it's within your control, you'll feel less pressure, you'll perform better, and as a result, you will probably win more.

> *"Michael Jordan told me once that you have to learn how to fail before you can learn to succeed."*
>
> **Shaquille O'Neal**

MYTH AND REALITY OF WINNING AND LOSING

There are many myths and misconceptions that athletes hold about winning and losing. Many athletes believe that the only way to win is to have always won; that winners rarely lose and losers always lose. The reality is that winners lose more often than losers. Losers lose a few times and quit. Winners lose at first, learn from the losses, then begin to win because of what they've learned.

Both winning and losing are essential to becoming a consistent winner. Winning builds confidence and reinforces athletes' belief that they can perform well, meet the challenges of competition, and defeat difficult opponents. There are, however, problems with winning too much and too early. Winning can breed complacency because, if athletes win all of the time, there's little motivation to improve. Sooner or later though, as athletes move up the competitive ladder, they'll come up against someone who is just as good or better than them, and since they haven't improved their performance, they won't be successful against them. Winning also doesn't identify areas in need of improvement. If athletes always win, their weaknesses won't become apparent and they won't see the need to work on their performance. Winning also doesn't teach athletes how to constructively handle the inevitable obstacles and setbacks of sport.

Athletes will be so accustomed to winning that when they finally do lose, it will be a shock to them.

There are also benefits to losing that will ultimately enable athletes to win more. Losing provides athletes with information about their progress. It shows athletes what you're doing well and, more importantly, what they need to improve on. Losing also shows athletes what doesn't work, which helps them identify what works best. Losing also teaches athletes how to positively handle adversity.

Rather than becoming discouraged by losing, you should focus on how it will help you become a better athlete. If you learn the valuable lessons from both winning and losing, you'll gain the perspective toward your sport that will allow you to achieve Prime Sport.

> *"Play tennis without fear of defeat and because it's fun or don't play at all. There is no disgrace in defeat. Champions are born in the labor of defeat."*
>
> **Tennis legend Bill Tilden**

PRIME SPORT COMPETITOR

Being the best athlete you can takes more than being in great physical condition and being technically skilled. There are many athletes who have those qualities, but don't perform to the best of their ability. There are many first-round draft picks who never became stars in their sport at the professional level. Performing your best requires that you have all of the normal things you would expect a great athlete to have: physically well-conditioned, excellent technique, sound tactics, and the latest equipment. That is not enough though; those things will only make you a good athlete. You need more to become your best. You need to become a Prime Sport competitor.

There's a big difference between being able to perform well in practice, during competitions, and in pressure situations. This difference is what separates athletes from Prime Sport competitors. It's difficult enough getting into good physical condition, developing good technical skills, and understanding the tactical aspects of your sport. The final challenge is learning how to evolve from an athlete to a Prime Sport competitor.

> *"I love to hit when the pressure's on. I enjoy the excitement. I try harder. I concentrate more."*
>
> **Reggie Jackson**

LEVELS OF COMPETITIVE SPORT

There are three levels at which you can compete. The first level is as an *athlete*. Athletes are technically solid and generally perform well in practice, but they don't usually perform up to their ability in competition. They perform even worse under pressure. Athletes typically only win when they are clearly more skilled than their opponents and never win big competitions.

The next level of performance is as a *performer*. Performers perform adequately in practice and perform well in most competitions. They can be counted on to win with some regularity. Performers, however, are rarely able to get that big win that propels them to top, and they almost never win big competitions. They don't respond well to the pressures of competition. They're unable to harness the pressure and raise their performances when the competition is on the line. Simply put, performers don't perform their best when it really counts.

The ultimate level is as a Prime Sport *competitor*. Prime Sport competitors don't always perform well in practice. They may even occasionally lose in less important competitions. But what separates Prime Sport competitors from athletes and performers is how they respond to

12   Prime Sport

pressure. In big competitions against tough opponents, their performances rise to a new level. Everything that turns negative for athletes and performers shifts positively for Prime Sport competitors. They thrive on the pressure of important competitions and perform their best against the most difficult opponents and in the worst conditions. Prime Sport competitors win the tough competitions that propel them to the top of their sport. Pete Sampras exemplifies the Prime Sport competitor. He sometimes loses in less important tournaments. When the Grand Slam events arrive though, he wins the tough matches and the big titles. That is what makes him one of the greatest athletes of all time.

QUALITIES OF A PRIME SPORT COMPETITOR

Looking back at the great competitors in sport over the years from Babe Didrikson and Jim Thorpe to Bill Russell and Chris Evert to Mia Hamm and Michael Johnson, you see in them common qualities that made them champions. Each had unique abilities, styles, and personalities, but all shared several essential characteristics.

At the heart of all Prime Sport competitors is an unwavering determination to be the best. They are driven to get better and better. They have a great passion for hard work. They spend hours training every day to improve their performance. They love the grind and repetition of training and they are willing to suffer to succeed. Most basically, their love of their sport precedes their love of competing and winning.

Prime Sport competitors have a deep and enduring belief in themselves. They have the confidence to take risks, to do seemingly impossible things, and to never give up no matter what. This belief enables them to be inspired rather than discouraged by defeat and allows them to keep faith in their ability even when they are not performing their best. Difficult conditions and tough competition are exciting challenges and opportunities to showcase their skills.

Prime Sport competitors are able to raise their performances when they need to in order to win. They seek out and thrive on the pressure of, for example, the Olympics, the World Series or the Super Bowl. They have the ability to stay calm and focused with a championship on the line. Most fundamentally, Prime Sport competitors perform their best in the most important competitions of their lives.

"In this league, the game is played from the shoulders up."

NFL quarterback Troy Aikman

HOW TO BECOME A PRIME SPORT COMPETITOR

Becoming a Prime Sport competitor requires that you maximize every aspect of your athletic ability. It starts at the physical level. You must be in the best possible physical condition of which you're capable. Next, you have to develop the technical side of your sport. You need to have your technique so well ingrained and automatic, that it holds up when the pressure is on. You must also be tactically skilled, knowing the best strategy for the competitive situation in which you find yourself. So far, though, this will only enable you to become a performer at best. It is the next step that will put you on the path to becoming a Prime Sport competitor.

You need to be highly motivated to put in the time and effort necessary to be physically, technically, and tactically prepared. You must develop the confidence that you can perform your best in the most important competition of your life under the most demanding conditions in which you have ever competed. You need to train yourself to seek out and thrive on pressure and have the ability to stay calm and focused when the competition is on the line. Lastly, you must have the ability to use your emotions to your advantage so that they help you to perform your best.

Prime Sport is devoted to helping you achieve this part of becoming a Prime Sport competitor. You must be totally prepared for every competition:

physically, technically, tactically, and mentally ready to perform your best. If you can develop yourself in these areas, you will become a Prime Sport competitor.

> *"I love feeling the pressure, I love it. I was telling my dad last night, 'There's no better position than being up front.'"*

> **Tiger Woods**

PRIME SPORT SKILLS ARE SKILLS

Many athletes have misconceptions about the mental side of sport. Athletes often believe that mental abilities are inborn, in other words, athletes either have them or they don't, and if not, they can't develop them. But mental abilities are skills, just like technical skills, that can be developed. You should approach Prime Sport skills the same way you approach physical and technical parts of your sport. If you work on them, your Prime Sport skills will improve and your overall sport performance will be raised.

> *"My physical skills may not be as good as they were in 1988, but my mental skills are so much better."*

> **Michael Jordan**

PRIME SPORT PYRAMID

This book is directed toward helping you experience the feeling and performance of Prime Sport. This goal is accomplished by ascending the Prime Sport pyramid, which is comprised of five essential mental factors that impact performance: motivation, confidence, intensity, focus, and emotions (see page 15). By developing these mental areas, you will achieve Prime Sport.

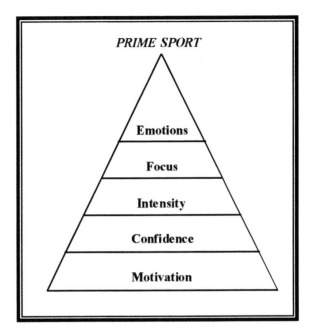

These five mental factors are ordered in a way that each area builds on the previous ones leading to Prime Sport. At the base of the Prime Sport pyramid lies motivation because without motivation there is no interest or desire to train. Prime motivation ensures that you put in the necessary time and effort to be totally prepared to perform your best. From motivation and preparation comes confidence in your physical, technical, and tactical capabilities, and in your ability to perform your best. Prime confidence gives you the desire to compete and the belief that you can win. From confidence comes the ability to manage your intensity and respond positively to the pressures of competition. Prime intensity enables you to consistently maintain your ideal level of intensity so you are physically capable of performing your best. From intensity comes the ability to focus properly during training and competition. Prime focus lets you stay focused and avoid distractions. From these four mental factors comes the ability to master your emotions. Prime emotions ensure that your emotions help rather than hurt your sport performances and that you are your best ally instead of your worst enemy while competing. Having ascended the Prime Sport pyramid, you will have the tools to achieve Prime Sport.

SECTION II:

PRIME SPORT ASSESSMENT

CHAPTER ONE

PRIME SPORT PROFILING

Now that you have an understanding of Prime Sport, you can begin the process of achieving it. The first step involves gaining a better understanding of yourself as an athlete. Self-understanding is so important because it shows you your strengths and areas in need of improvement and enables you to realize how you react in certain situations. This self-understanding then results in more efficient change. Becoming the best athlete you can is complicated. You probably have a busy life filled with sports, school, work, family, social life, and other activities. It's difficult to find time to do everything. By understanding yourself, you'll know what you need to work on to be efficient and focused in your efforts.

In developing greater self-understanding, athletes must recognize their strengths and weaknesses. Most athletes love to focus on their strengths, but don't like to admit that they have weaknesses. This attitude will limit their development. Most athletes think that they're as good as their greatest strengths. For example, an offensive lineman in football believes that his size and strength advantage enables him to be successful. The truth is, however, that athletes are only as good as their biggest weakness. Returning to that example, if the opposing defensive lineman is very quick, the offensive lineman's size and strength can be neutralized and his lack of speed will determine the outcome of match-up.

Think of athletic strengths and weaknesses as a mathematical equation (see Prime Profile Formula below). If a basketball player is a very good shooter (10), but she is not a good defender (2), her overall performance would be low (10+2=12). If she worked on and improved your defense (7), then her overall performance would rise significantly (10+7=17). The more athletes improve their weaknesses, the higher their overall performances will be and the more they will win.

PRIME PROFILE FORMULA

Strengths + Weaknesses = Overall Sport Performance

WHY PRIME SPORT PROFILING?

A difficulty with dealing with the mental aspects of sport is that they're not tangible or easily measured. If you want to learn what are your physical strengths and weaknesses, you can go through a physical testing program that gives you objective data about your physical condition. Think of Prime Sport profiling as physical testing for the mind. It makes mental issues related to your sport more concrete. Prime Sport profiling increases your self-understanding so you can take active steps to maintain your strengths and improve your weaknesses.

It's important for you to have an open mind with Prime Sport profiling. Rather than being uncomfortable with facing your weaknesses, you should be willing to consider the information in a positive and constructive way. When weaknesses are identified, it doesn't mean that you're incapable of performing well. It may be that you haven't had to use these skills at your current level or you've been able to hide them with the strengths you have.

"As you grow up, you learn more about yourself, I tried to...learn about myself and my weaknesses and strengths."

Olympic skiing champion Lasse Kjus

COMPLETING THE PRIME SPORT PROFILE

The Prime Sport profile (see page 23) is comprised of 12 mental, emotional, and competitive factors that impact sports performance. To complete the Prime Sport profile, read the description of each factor and rate yourself on a one-to-ten scale by drawing a line at that level and shading in the area toward the center of the profile.

Motivation refers to how determined you are to train and compete to achieve your athletic goals. Motivation affects all aspects of your preparation including your desire to put time and energy into physical conditioning, technical and tactical development, and mental preparation. Do you work consistently hard on all aspects of your sport or do you give up when you get tired, bored, or frustrated? (1-not at all motivated; 10-very motivated)

Confidence relates to how positive or negative your self-talk and body language are during competition. It includes how well you're able to maintain your confidence during competitions, especially difficult ones. Do you stay positive even under pressure and when you're not performing well or do you become negative and get down on yourself? (1-very negative; 10-very positive)

Intensity involves whether your physical intensity helps or hurts your performances. In pressure situations, are you able to maintain a level of intensity that allows you to perform well or do you become too anxious to perform well? (1-hurts, anxious; 10-helps, just right)

Focus is concerned with how well you're able to keep your mind on performing your best during competition. It involves avoiding distractions and not losing focus in difficult competitions. Are you able to stay focused on what you need to in order to perform well or do you become distracted by things that hurt your performances? (1-distracted; 10-focused)

Emotions involve how well you're able to control your emotions during a competition. Particularly in difficult competitions or when you're not performing well, do you stay positive and excited or do you get angry, depressed, or frustrated? Simply put, do your emotions help or hurt you during competitions? (1-lose control, hurt; 10-have control, help)

Consistency relates to how well you're able to maintain your level of performance during a competition. Does your level of performance stay at a consistently high level or does it go up and down frequently during a competition? (1-very inconsistent; 10-very consistent)

Routines involve how much you use routines in your sport. Do you have a pre-competitive routine to prepare for an event? Do you have a routine between performances? How consistent are you in using routines in your sport? (1-never; 10-often)

Competitor refers to how well you perform in competition as compared to practice. Do you perform better, the same, or worse in competitions as compared to practice? (1-not as well; 10-better)

Adversity is concerned with your ability to respond positively to difficulties you're faced with during competitions. For example, how do you react when the conditions are poor or your opponent is tough? (1-decline; 10-improve)

Pressure relates to your ability to perform your best in difficult competitive situations such as when the competition is on the line or time is running out. Does your performance improve or does it decline when the competition is on the line? (1-poorly; 10-well)

Ally involves whether you are your best ally or your worst enemy during a competition. Are you positive and encouraging to yourself or do you get angry and berate yourself, especially when you're behind or not performing well? (1-enemy; 10-ally)

Prime Sport refers to how often you achieve and maintain your highest level of performance. Are you able to achieve Prime Sport regularly or is it a rare occurrence for you? (1-never; 10-often)

PRIME SPORT PROFILE

Name _____   **Date** _____

Directions: Twelve mental factors that impact sports performance are identified in the profile below. Using the definitions provided above, rate yourself on a 1-10 scale for each factor by drawing a line at that level and shading in the area toward   the center of profile. A score below a   <u>7</u> indicates an area in need of improvement.

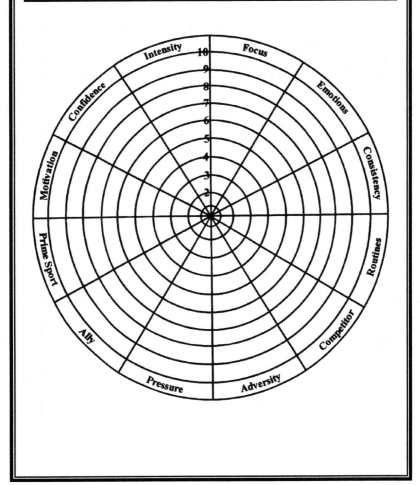

USING YOUR PRIME SPORT PROFILE

Having completed the Prime Sport profile, you now have a clear picture of what you believe to be the mental strengths and weaknesses in your sport. Typically, a score below a 7 indicates an area on which you need to work. Place a **T** next to each factor that you scored as less than a 7. These are the factors that you'll want to consider working on in your Prime Sport program.

From those checked factors, select three to focus on in the immediate future. It doesn't make sense to deal with every one that you need to strengthen. You'll just become overloaded and won't give adequate attention to any of them. It's best to focus on a few, strengthen them, then move on to others.

The question is, if you have more than three factors on which you need to work, which ones should you choose? The decision should be based on several concerns. First, you should look at which ones are most important for your long-term development. Just like working on the physical and technical aspects of your sport, you should focus on the factors that will help you in the long run. Second, some weaknesses are symptoms of other weaknesses. By dealing with one factor, another one can be relieved without having to work on it directly. For example, you may not handle pressure well because you lack confidence. By building your confidence, you also improve your ability to handle pressure. Third, you need to balance your immediate training and competitive needs with your long-term development. You may have an important competition coming up for which you need to be ready. For example, you may decide that you need to improve your focus and intensity immediately even though working on your motivation and confidence will be more important in the future.

Using the Prime Sport Priority form (see page 25), indicate the three mental factors you want to focus on in the near future. After reading *Prime Sport*, return to the relevant chapters to learn about techniques and exercises that will help you strengthen the areas you've selected. Use the goal setting and Prime Sport program described in Section V to work on those areas.

You can also use Prime Sport Profiling to measure progress in your training. Periodically, perhaps once a month, complete the profile and compare it with your past profiles. You should see improvement in the areas on which you've worked. Also, ask your coaches about positive changes they've seen in those areas. When your ratings move above 7, select other factors to work on and follow the same procedure.

> *"A part of greatness is learning to correct your weaknesses. The first thing is to know your faults and then take on a systematic plan of correcting them."*

> **Babe Ruth**

PRIME SPORT PRIORITY

Name _____   Date _____

Directions: In the space below, indicate three areas that you have identified in your Prime Sport profile on which you would like to focus in your sport. As these areas improve and new areas need work, complete this form again to specify the new priorities.

1.

2.

3.

SECTION III:

PRIME SPORT PYRAMID

CHAPTER TWO

MOTIVATION

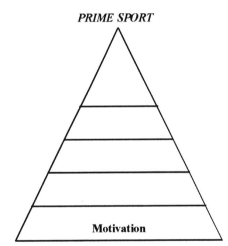

PRIME SPORT

Motivation

Motivation lies at the base of the Prime Sport pyramid. Without athletes' desire and determination to improve their sports performances, all of the other mental factors, confidence, intensity, focus, and emotions, are meaningless. To become the best athlete they can be, they must be motivated to do what it takes to maximize their ability.

Motivation, simply defined, is the ability to initiate and persist at a task. To perform their best, athletes must want to begin the process of developing as an athlete and they must be willing to maintain their efforts until they have achieved their goals. Motivation in sports is so important because athletes must be willing to work hard in the face of fatigue, boredom, pain, and the desire to do other things. Motivation will impact everything that influences sports performance: physical conditioning, technical and tactical training, mental preparation, and general lifestyle including sleep, diet, school or work, and relationships.

The reason motivation is so important is that it is the only contributor to sports performance over which athletes have control. My Performance Formula (see below) helps explain this notion. There are three things that affect how well athletes perform. First, their ability, which includes their physical, technical, tactical, and mental capabilities, impacts their level of performance. Though these four factors can change over time with practice, on any given day, athletes can not alter them dramatically. For example, a basketball player is not going to improve her free throw shooting the day of a game enough for it to result in better free throw shooting. Whatever athletes bring to the competition in terms of their ability is what they will have to use that day. In the short-run, athletes have little real control over their ability.

PERFORMANCE FORMULA

Ability - Difficulty of Competition + Motivation = PERFORMANCE

Second, the difficulty of the competition influences performance. Contributors to difficulty include the ability of the opponent and external factors such as an "away game" crowd and weather such as temperature, wind, and sun. Athletes have no control over these factors.

Finally, motivation will impact performance. Motivation will directly affect athletes' long-term development and the level that athletes ultimately achieve. If athletes are highly motivated to improve their performances, then they will put in the time and effort necessary to raise their game. Motivation will also influence the level of performance when athletes begin a competition. If they're competing against someone of nearly equal skill, it will not be ability that will determine the outcome. Rather, it will be the athlete who works the hardest, who doesn't give up, and who performs their best when it counts. In other words, the athlete who is most motivated to win.

"With motivation, you can be involved or committed.
Just like with ham and eggs: the chicken was involved,
but the pig was committed. You have to be like the pig."

Martina Navratilova

SIGNS OF LOW MOTIVATION

Two questions athletes must ask themselves are, "How motivated am I?" and "Am I as motivated as I can be?" There are some common signs of low motivation. A lack of desire to practice as much as athletes could is one clear symptom of low motivation. This is especially important if their goals are high. Goals are great to have, but they will be unfulfilled if athletes are not motivated to achieve them. It's very important that motivation be consistent with goals. Are you willing to do what is necessary to reach your goals? If not, then you have two choices: increase your motivation so you can attain your goals or lower your goals to a level that, given your motivation, you will be able to reach.

Less than 100% effort in training is another warning sign of low motivation. When you train, do you give it your all? Do you work as hard as you can when you're practicing? Or do you not try that hard and put less than complete effort into your training? Skipping or shortening training sessions is also common for athletes with low motivation. If athletes are not motivated, it's easy to skip practice because they just don't feel like it. If they do go to practice, they may only stay for a little while or they may goof around more than they practice. If you exhibit any of these symptoms of low motivation, you're not going to be the best athlete you can be. If you're not as motivated as you could be, you have to do two things. First, ask yourself why you're not working as hard as you could. Second, you must take active steps to increase your motivation in your sport.

"You've got to care. You start uncovering the layers of everything surrounding the game—the money, the hype, the stardom—and it comes down to this: How bad do you want it?"

NFL player Carnell Lake

PRIME MOTIVATION

Prime motivation means putting 100% of your time, effort, energy, and focus into all aspects of your sport. It involves doing everything possible to become the best athlete you can be. Prime motivation is based on what I call the three D's (see below). The first D stands for *direction*. Before you can attain prime motivation, you must first consider the different directions you can go in your sport. You have three choices: stop participating completely, continue at your current level, or strive to be the best athlete you can be.

The second D represents *decision*. With these three choices of direction, you must select one direction in which to go. None of these directions are necessarily right or wrong, better or worse, they're simply your options. Your choice will dictate the amount of time and effort you will put into your sport and how good an athlete you will ultimately become.

The third D stands for *dedication*. Once you've made your decision, you must dedicate yourself to it. If your decision is to become the best athlete you can be, then this last step, dedication, will determine whether you have prime motivation. Your decision to be your best and your dedication to your sport must be a top priority. Only by being completely dedicated to your direction and decision will you ensure that you have prime motivation.

THREE D'S

Direction → Decision → Dedication → MOTIVATION

DEVELOPING PRIME MOTIVATION

Focus on your long-term goals. To be your best, you have to put a lot of time and effort into your sport. But all of that time and effort is not always enjoyable. I call this the *Grind*, which involves having to put hours upon hours of time into training, well beyond the point that it is fun and exciting. If you let these immediate negative aspects of your sport override the long-term benefits of working hard and putting in the time, your motivation is going to suffer and you're not going to get the most out of your sport.

During those times when your motivation is lagging, focus on your long-term goals. Remind yourself why you're working so hard. Imagine exactly what you want to accomplish and tell yourself that the only way you'll be able to reach your goals is to go through the Grind. Also, try to generate the feelings of joy and fulfillment that you will experience when you reach your goals. This technique will distract you from the unpleasantness of the Grind, focus you on what you want to achieve, and generate positive thoughts and emotions that will get you through the Grind.

Have a training partner. It's difficult to be highly motivated all of the time on your own. There are going to be some days when you don't feel like getting out there. Also, no matter how hard you push yourself, you will work that much harder if you have someone pushing you. That someone can be a coach, personal trainer, or parent. However, the best person to have is a regular training partner. A training partner is someone at about your level of ability and with similar goals. You can work together to accomplish your goals. The chances are on any given day that one of you will be motivated. Even if you're not very psyched to practice on a particular day, you will still put in the time and effort because your partner is counting on you.

Focus on greatest competitor. Another way to keep yourself motivated is to focus on your greatest competitor. I have athletes identify who their biggest competition is and put his or her name or photo where they can see it every day. Ask yourself, "Am I working as hard as him/her?" Remember that only by working your hardest will you have a chance to overcome your greatest competitor.

Motivational cues. A big part of staying motivated involves generating positive emotions associated with your efforts and achieving your goals. A way to keep those feelings is with motivational cues such as inspirational phrases and photographs. If you come across a quote or a picture that moves you, place it where you can see it regularly such as in your bedroom, on your refrigerator door, or in your locker. Look at it periodically and allow yourself to experience the emotions it creates in you. These reminders and the emotions associated with them will inspire and motivate you to work hard in your sport.

Set goals. There are few things more rewarding and motivating than setting a goal, putting effort toward the goal, and achieving the goal. The sense of accomplishment and validation of the effort makes you feel good and motivates you to strive higher. It's valuable to establish clear goals of what you want to accomplish in your sport and how you will achieve those goals. Section V will describe how to do just that. Seeing that your hard work leads to progress and results should motivate you further to realize your sport goals.

Daily questions. Finally, every day, you should ask yourself two questions. When you get up in the morning, ask, "What can I do today to become the best athlete I can be?" and before you go to sleep, ask, "Did I do everything possible today to become the best athlete I can be?" These two questions will remind you daily of what your goal is and will challenge you to be motivated to become your best.

The heart of motivation. A final point about motivation. The techniques I've just described are effective in increasing your motivation. Motivation, though, is not something that can be given to you. Rather, motivation must ultimately come from within. You must simply want to participate in your sport. Motivation won't be a problem if you compete for the right reasons.

There are two things that should motivate you to compete. First, you should compete because you have a great passion for your sport. If you love your sport, you will be motivated to perform to best of your ability.

Second, you should perform because you love the process of your sport. Not the winning, not the trophies, not the rankings, though they can certainly make you feel good. You should compete because you just love to get out there and do it. There are not many professional athletes who don't love the Grind. It is that love that helps make them successful. If you truly love your sport, your motivation to work at all aspects of performance will be high.

> *"[Michael] Jordan now wins with qualities that all of us have within us somewhere: work ethic, drive, competitiveness, and will."*
> **Sports writer John Feinstein**

TWELVE LAWS OF PRIME PREPARATION

By achieving prime motivation, you take the first and most crucial step toward reaching your sport goals. You can now follow what I call the Prime Motivation Progression (see below). Prime motivation pushes you to put in the necessary time and effort to be the best athlete you can be. This time and effort ensures that you have prime preparation, which I define as doing everything you can to be fully prepared to perform your best.

PRIME MOTIVATION PROGRESSION

Prime Motivation → Prime Preparation → Prime Sport

It is preparation that acts as the bridge between prime motivation and Prime Sport. Without preparation, you will not have the tools or the experience to achieve your sport goals. From my years of working with athletes at all levels of ability, I have developed twelve laws that must be understood and followed in order to accomplish prime preparation and achieve Prime Sport.

First Law: *Competitions are not won on the day you compete, but rather in the days, weeks, and months before the competition.* Many athletes believe that if they're ready to go on the day of a competition, then they will prepared to perform their best. But I have found that success is determined more by what you do in the days, weeks, and months leading up to the competition. If you've put in the time and effort to develop your physical, technical, tactical, and mental abilities, you will have the skills and the belief to perform your best on the day of the competition.

Second Law: *Take responsibility for everything that can impact your performance.* The only way that prime preparation can be achieved is if you know every area that influences your sport performance. These areas include all of the components of physical, technical, tactical, and mental preparation. If you address every one of these areas, you can be sure that when you get to the competition, you will be totally prepared to perform your best.

Third Law: *Preparation is the foundation of all physical, technical, tactical, and mental skills.* There is no magic to acquiring skills. There are no special techniques that enable you to learn faster or better. Developing skills of any sort requires three steps: (1) Awareness of what you're doing incorrectly and what is the proper execution; (2) Control to engage in the skills correctly; and (3) Repetition to ingrain the new skills. Only with this preparation will you be able to use those skills effectively and with confidence in a competition.

Fourth Law: *The purpose of training is to develop effective skills.* Training will ingrain in you a variety of physical, technical, tactical, and mental skills. If you want to perform your best, you must be sure that you're developing skills that will facilitate rather than interfere with Prime Sport. Whatever you practice, those are the skills that you will learn. If you practice effective skills, you'll develop skills that will help you perform your best. If you practice poor skills, you'll become good at those and they will hurt your performance. It's important that you're always practicing physical, technical, tactical, and mental skills that will allow you to achieve Prime Sport.

Fifth Law: *Athletes should train like they compete.* Whenever I give a seminar to athletes or coaches, I ask this question: Should you train like you compete or should you compete like you train? Most say, you should compete like you train. Their response is understandable in some ways because if you could compete in the positive, relaxed, and focused way that you train, then you would certainly perform well. I believe that competing like you train is impossible for one simple reason: competition matters. Training is easy because you don't care that much how you perform. If you perform poorly in competitions, you do care.

The problem is that many athletes train at 60-70%, then expect to be able to jump to 100% motivation, focus, and intensity in a competition and perform their best. Unfortunately, this leap is too great and they perform poorly. Training like you compete means putting as close to the same level of motivation, focus, and intensity into training as you do in a competition. It's probably unrealistic to think that you can train exactly like you compete. If you can get close to it, say 90%, then the last 10% that comes in a competition will be an easy step up.

Sixth Law: *Prime preparation requires clear purpose, prime focus, and prime intensity.* It's impossible to engage in quality training unless three things are present. You must have a clear purpose that tells you what you're working on. If you don't know what you're doing to improve, you won't be able to work on it. Identifying the purpose of your preparation ensures that you put directed effort into that purpose.

You must have prime focus which involves consistently maintaining focus on your purpose and avoiding distractions that will interfere with that focus. This means having cues to focus on that remind you of your purpose and ways of redirecting your focus when you become distracted.

You must have prime intensity to achieve prime preparation. All of the mental techniques in the world won't work if your body is not prepared to execute the purpose you have identified. Having the awareness and control of your intensity will enable your body to ingrain the purpose and focus that you have worked on.

Seventh Law: *Consistent training leads to consistent competitive performance.* Consistency is essential to Prime Sport and is one of the most important qualities that put the best athletes above the rest. The consistency in Prime Sport comes from consistency in training. Referring back to my fourth law, consistency is one of those effective skills that you need to develop in order to achieve Prime Sport. Consistency relates to every aspects of sport training and life. In addition to the obvious areas such as conditioning, technique, and tactics, it also pertains to attitude, effort, focus, intensity, emotions, sleep, and diet. Any area that influences your performance must be consistent before you can be consistent in a competition.

Eighth Law: *Patience and persistence are essential to achieving Prime Sport.* Skills take time to develop and you will experience plateaus, setbacks, and obstacles along the path toward Prime Sport. You may get frustrated, impatient, and want to quit. If you let frustration and impatience overwhelm you, you will never achieve Prime Sport. If you understand that progress takes time and that there is no way to hurry the learning process, you will have the patience to develop Prime Sport. Drawing on that patience, if you persist long enough in the face of setbacks and obstacles, the improvement will come and you will achieve Prime Sport.

Ninth Law: *Failure is essential for Prime Sport.* Many athletes believe that failure, in the form of mistakes and poor results, is something to be avoided. If you fail, then you're a failure. If you fail, then you will never be successful. But there can not be success without failure. Failure shows you what is not working. It means that you are moving out of your comfort zone. Failure means you are taking risks. Failure teaches you how to deal positively with adversity.

Tenth Law: *Prime Sport comes from "one more thing, one more time."* You can assume that most of your competitors are working hard to become the best athletes they can be. If you want to defeat them, you must ask yourself, "What can I do to get the edge over them?" Here is a simple rule I learned from Bernard Russi, 1972 Olympic downhill skiing champion: "One more thing, one more time." When you feel you have done enough, you should do one more drill, do one more set of weights, or do one more wind sprint. By doing one more thing, one more time, you are doing that little bit extra that will separate you on the day of the competition.

Eleventh Law: *It takes 10 years and 10,000 hours to become a great athlete.* Research that has studied expert performance in sports, music, chess, and other areas found two things that predict the level that someone will achieve: how long they've been committed to the activity and how much they trained. Applied to sports, the longer you have been in your sport and the more hours you have trained, the better you will be. Ten years and 10,000 hours comes out about 20 hours per week of commitment to your sport.

Twelfth Law: *Prime preparation is devoted to readying athletes to perform their best under the most demanding conditions in the most important competition of their life.* I'm not interested in you performing well in unimportant competitions, under ideal conditions, against a field that you know you can defeat. The ultimate goal of Prime Sport is for you perform your best when it really counts. Prime preparation will allow you to achieve Prime Sport in your equivalent of the Super Bowl, Olympics, or soccer World Cup.

> *"For me, winning isn't something that happens suddenly on the field when the whistle blows and crowds roar. Winning is something that builds physically and mentally every day that you train and every night that you dream."*
>
> **NFL running back Emmitt Smith**

CHAPTER THREE

CONFIDENCE

PRIME SPORT

Confidence

Motivation

Confidence is the single most important mental factor for success in sports. I define confidence as how strongly you believe you can perform your best. Confidence impacts two levels of your sport: your ability to perform in your sport and your ability to win. Confidence is so important because you may have all of the ability in the world to perform well, but if you don't believe you have that ability, then you won't perform up to that ability. For example, a gymnast may be physically and technically capable of executing a double-back somersault with a full twist on the floor exercise, but he won't attempt the skill if doesn't have the confidence that he can successfully execute the skill.

Have you ever seen athletes in a sport who compete at a high level, but are not considered among the best? For example, a basketball player who plays in a European professional league rather than the NBA or a tennis pro who is ranked around 200 in the world. If not, what you would see are outstanding athletes with exceptional skills in most facets of their sport.

What separates these athletes from those who are considered to be the best in their sport if they seem to have similar skills at their disposal? It is often not their physical or technical capabilities but rather their belief in their ability to perform at a critical time in the most important competition of their lives. The best athletes have the confidence that they will perform their best and be successful when it really counts. The lower ranked athletes don't have that confidence, so they won't, for example, go for the three-point shot with the game on the line or try to hit an offensive lob at match point against them.

Too often athletes are their own worst enemy rather than their best ally. Have you ever seen professional athletes who seem to turn on themselves? They get frustrated and angry, and these negative reactions cause them to lose. Albert Belle and Dennis Rodman come to mind.

Whether you're your best ally or your worst enemy depends on your confidence. If you don't have much confidence in yourself, you probably don't think you can perform your best and win. If that's the case and your opponent has confidence, then you're in an impossible situation. As your worst enemy, you don't have a chance because it's two against zero; you and your opponent against you. The only way you have the chance to win is to become your best ally so that at least it is one against one. You have to allow yourself to be on your own side. Only then will you have any chance of performing well and winning.

> *"I have no secret. I just feel very confident, and that allows me to take all the risks I want and to push all the way down the hill."*
>
> **World Cup skiing champion Michael Von Greunigen**

VICIOUS CYCLE OR UPWARD SPIRAL

Not only does confidence impact performance directly, it also affects every other mental factor. To help illustrate this influence of confidence, think back to a time when you didn't have confidence in your sport. You probably got caught in a vicious cycle of low confidence and performance in which negative thinking led to poor performance, which led to more negative thinking and even poorer performance until your confidence was so low that you didn't even want to compete (see page 47).

This vicious cycle usually starts with a period of poor performance or some losses. This poor performance can lead to negative thinking and self-talk. "I'm terrible. I can't do this. I don't have a chance. I can't win today." You are becoming your own worst enemy.

You start to get nervous before a competition because you believe you will lose. All of that anxiety hurts your confidence even more because you feel physically uncomfortable and there's no way you can perform well when you're so uptight. The negative self-talk and anxiety causes negative emotions. You feel depressed, frustrated, angry, and helpless, all of which hurt your confidence more and cause you to perform even worse.

The negative self-talk, anxiety, and emotions then hurt your focus. If you have low confidence, you can't help but focus on all of the negative things rather than on things that will enable you to perform your best. All of this accumulated negativity hurts your motivation. As bad as you feel, you just want to get out of there. If you're thinking negatively, caught in a vicious cycle, feeling nervous, depressed, and frustrated, and can't focus, you're not going to have much fun and you're not going to perform well.

In contrast to those times when you have had low confidence, recall when you have been really confident in your sport. Your self-talk is positive. "I'm a good athlete. I can perform well. I can win." Instead of being your worst enemy, you're your best ally.

With the positive self-talk, rather than being dragged down into the vicious cycle, you begin an upward spiral of high confidence and performance in which positive thinking leads to better performance, which leads to more positive thinking and even better performance (see page 47).

All of the positive talk gets you feeling relaxed and energized as you begin the competition. You have a lot of positive emotions such as happiness, joy and excitement. You focus on things you need to perform your best. Competing is actually an enjoyable experience for you.

All of the positive thoughts and feelings motivate you to perform. If you're thinking positively, riding an upward spiral, feeling relaxed and energized, experiencing happiness and excitement, and are focused on performing your best, you're going to have a lot of fun and you're going to perform well.

> *"I felt lower than low. I stood on the sideline asking myself, Am I the worst quarterback ever to play here?"*
>
> **BYU quarterback Kevin Feterik**

WHY ATHLETES LOSE CONFIDENCE

Remember that confidence is the belief athletes have in their ability to perform well. Anything that counters that belief will hurt their confidence. The most disruptive thing to hurt confidence is failure of any kind. Failure can mean making mistakes in a competition, for example, missing an easy header in soccer or falling on a double axel in figure skating. Failure will cause athletes to lose confidence in themselves and cause them to become tentative or cautious. Failure can also mean having poor results in recent competitions. Athletes who have performed poorly may question their ability and may become unwilling to take risks and push themselves hard.

Unrealistic expectations can also hurt confidence. You should make sure that your confidence is realistic. In other words, is your confidence in your ability consistent with your actual ability? If it is not, then you'll have unrealistic expectations that can never be reached. You may be overly critical of your performances based on those unreasonable beliefs about your ability, believing that you didn't perform as well as you should have instead of simply having performed up to your realistic ability.

Lack of experience or skills can also hurt confidence. If you have not competed very much or have not performed at the current level in which you're now competing, you may not have the experience to adequately evaluate how well you should perform. Often, performances that are interpreted as poor are actually just the opponent performing at a higher level. This is particularly likely if you're performing at a new level above where you had previously competed. You may simply lack the necessary experience to be competitive at that level. Without this realization, instead of adjusting your perceptions accordingly, you'll assume that you're performing poorly and your confidence will decline.

> *"I eliminate any kind of negative thinking. You succeed as a major league player because you have to believe in yourself."*
>
> **Major League Baseball player Brady Anderson**

CONFIDENCE IS A SKILL

A misconception that many athletes have is that confidence is something that is inborn or that if they don't have it at an early age, they will never have confidence. In reality, confidence is a skill, much like technical skills, that can be learned. Just like with any type of skill, confidence is developed through practice and experience.

The problem many athletes have with confidence is that they violate my fourth law of preparation. They developed ineffective confidence skills, and by practicing being negative, they became skilled at being negative. These athletes became highly skilled at something that actually hurts their sports performance.

If an athlete has a bad technical habit, for example, a softball player opens her shoulders too early when swinging, she probably has swung the bat that way for a long time. She has become skilled at swinging the bat the wrong way. The same holds true for confidence. Athletes can become skilled at being negative.

To change bad confidence skills, athletes must retrain the way they think. They have to practice good confidence skills regularly until the old negative habits have been broken and they have learned and ingrained the new positive skills of confidence. The techniques described below will help you in this process by giving you specific strategies you can use to unlearn bad habits and learn good skills.

A question I'm often asked is, "Do you become confident by succeeding or do you succeed from being confident?" I believe that success in sports comes from confidence. You don't just go from 0% confidence to 100% confidence in one big step. Rather, it's a building process in which confidence leads to success which reinforces the confidence which, in turn, leads to more success. For example, a football placekicker may only have 40% confidence in his ability to kick field goals longer than 30 yards. By working on his technique and his physical conditioning and using the confidence-building techniques described on the following pages, his confidence goes up to 60%. Yet, all of the positive thinking in the world won't help if he doesn't have experiences to confirm his beliefs. With his confidence now at 60%, the placekicker is able to have greater focus and intensity in his training, which results in improved technique and greater distance on his kicks. His hard work and progress raise his confidence to 80%. His improved preparation and greater confidence results in more distance and consistency in practice. His improved kicking and his success in practice then increases his confidence to near 100%, enabling him to kick in games with confidence and success.

"Do I lose confidence? Never. That's what separates the good players from the bad players."

Charles Barkley

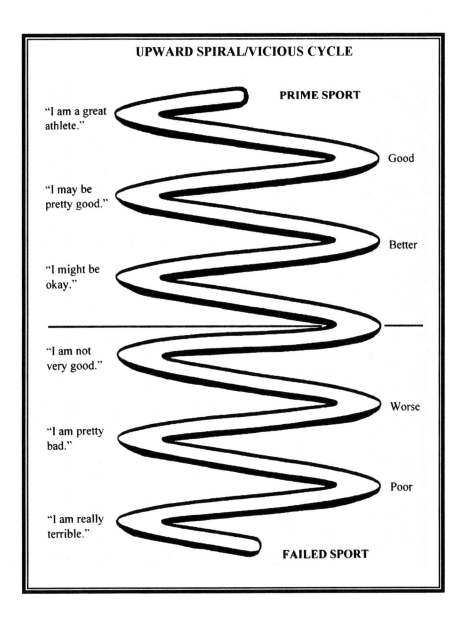

PRIME CONFIDENCE

Prime confidence is a deep, lasting, and resilient belief in one's ability. With prime confidence, athletes are able to stay confident even when they're not performing well. Prime confidence keeps them positive, motivated, intense, focused, and emotionally in control when they need to be. Athletes are not negative and uncertain in difficult competitions and they're not overconfident in easy competitions. It also encourages athletes to seek out pressure situations and to view difficult conditions and tough opponents as challenges to pursue. Prime confidence enables athletes to perform at their highest level consistently.

Prime confidence is a belief, not a certainty, that athletes can win. It is the confidence that if athletes do the right things, they will prevail. Prime confidence demonstrates faith and trust in their ability and their preparation. It does not, however, lead athletes to know, expect, or have to win. This belief can produce arrogance and overconfidence. It can also cause athletes to become too focused on winning the competition instead of performing their best in the competition. This perception can lead to self-imposed pressure and a fear of losing.

> *"If you have the skills and the confidence, then you do things at your own level. You don't worry about the level of other people."*
>
> **Earl Woods speaking of his son Tiger**

PROGRESSION OF CONFIDENCE

I have identified a four-step progression that will lead you along the upward spiral of confidence. Each step alone can enhance your confidence, but if you use all of them together, you'll find your confidence growing stronger and more quickly. The ultimate goal of prime confidence is to develop a strong and resilient belief in your athletic ability so that you have the confidence to give your best effort, perform at your highest level, and believe you can win the most important competitions of your life.

Preparation breeds confidence. Preparation is the foundation of confidence. If you believe that you have done everything you can to perform your best, you will have confidence in your ability to perform well. This preparation includes the physical, technical, tactical, and mental parts of your sport. If you have developed these areas as fully as you can, you will have faith that you will be able to use those skills gained from preparation to perform as well as you can. The more of these areas you cover in your preparation, the more confidence you will breed in yourself.

Mental skills reinforce confidence. As I have indicated previously, confidence is a skill that develops with practice. A meaningful way to strengthen the confidence you've built through preparation is to use mental skills that provide repetition of the confidence. These mental skills include goal setting to bolster motivation, positive self-talk and body language to fortify the confident beliefs, intensity control to combat confidence-depleting anxiety, keywords to maintain focus and avoid distractions, and emotional control to stay calm under pressure. These mental skills are described throughout Section III.

Adversity ingrains confidence. It's one thing to be confident when you're performing well and things are going your way. It is an entirely different challenge to maintain your belief in yourself when you're faced with adversity. To more deeply ingrain confidence in your sport, you should expose yourself to as much adversity as possible. Adversity can involve anything that makes you uncomfortable and takes you out of your comfort zone. Adversity can be environmental obstacles such as bad weather including rain during soccer game or poor competitive conditions such as an unfriendly crowd at a hockey game. Adversity can also involve your opponent, for example, someone who is a little better than you are, or an opponent who has a style of play that frustrates you, or someone who you believe you should defeat but who always seems to get the better of you.

Performing under adversity has several essential benefits. It demonstrates your competence to perform well under difficult conditions. Adversity teaches you additional skills you can use to perform at a higher level. It also prepares you for adversity that you will inevitably experience when you perform in important competitions. All of these aspects of adversity will ingrain confidence in your sport.

Success validates confidence. All of the previous steps in building confidence would go for naught if you did not then perform well and win. Success validates the confidence you have developed in your ability. It demonstrates that your belief in your ability is well-founded. Success further strengthens your confidence, making it more resilient in the face of adversity and poor performance. Finally, success rewards your efforts to build confidence, encouraging you to continue to work hard and develop your performance.

> *"The most progressive thing I have seen on the field is the attitude of the team. The players believe they can win. They're playing like winners, they're acting like winners, they're talking like winners."*
>
> **Former New York Yankee manager Billy Martin**

BUILDING PRIME CONFIDENCE

You now see the importance of having prime confidence. Let's discuss how you can develop your confidence with Prime Sport techniques. One mistake that athletes often make is they wait to do mental training until after they've lost confidence. You don't wait to get hurt before you start doing physical training. You don't wait to develop a technical problem before you work on technique. You do them beforehand to prevent the problems. The same thing holds true for building confidence.

Walk the walk. One thing I've noticed about working with world-class and professional athletes is that they carry themselves a certain way. They move and walk with confidence. A first step in developing confidence is to learn to "walk the walk." How you carry yourself, move, and walk affects what you think and how you feel. If your body is down, your thoughts and feelings will be negative. If your body is up, your thoughts and feelings will be positive. It's hard to feel down when your body is up. Walking the walk involves moving with your head high, chin up, eyes forward, shoulders back, arms swinging, and a bounce in your step. You look and move like a winner.

In contrast, not walking the walk involves your head, eyes, and shoulders down, feet dragging, and no energy in your step. You look and move like a loser. To give you a feeling of what this is like, try walking the walk and saying negative things about yourself. As you will see, it's difficult to do because your thoughts are inconsistent with what your body is signaling to you. Then try not walking the walk and saying positive things. Again, it's difficult because your thoughts conflict with what your body is doing.

Related to walking the walk, you can influence your thoughts and feelings with your body language. To get more positive, clench your fist, pump your arms, slap your thigh. This positive body language will affect your thinking and emotions, especially if you combine it with high-energy positive self-talk.

By the way, when you walk the walk, not only are you telling yourself that you're confident, but you're also communicating confidence to your opponent. There's nothing more discouraging than to be ahead, but to see an opponent who is positive, fired up, and motivated to keep fighting. There is also nothing more invigorating than to see your opponent looking like they've already lost. By not walking the walk, you're not only hurting your confidence, but you're also building your opponent's confidence.

Talk the talk. In addition to walking the walk, you can also learn to "talk the talk." What you say to yourself affects what you think and how you feel. If your talk is negative, your thoughts and feelings will be negative. If your talk is positive, your thoughts and feelings will be positive. It's hard to think and feel negative when you're talking positively. Don't say, "I don't have a chance today." Say, "I'm going to try my hardest today. I'm going to perform the best I can." That will get you positive and fired up. By talking the talk, you're also being your own best ally. You're showing yourself that your opponent may be against you, but you're on your side. If you're saying positive things out loud during a competition, you're also letting your opponent know that if you're going to lose, they will have to defeat you, you will not defeat yourself.

Conversely, not talking the talk includes "I'm going to perform terribly today," "I may do okay," and "I don't know how I'll do today." If you say these things to yourself, you're convincing yourself that you have little chance. With that attitude, you really have no chance because not only is your opponent planning on defeating you, but you're planning on losing to them as well. Even worse, if you talk negatively out loud during a competition, you're basically saying to your opponent that you've already lost.

Balance the scales. When I work with athletes, I always chart the number of positive and negative things they say or do during a competition. In most cases, the negatives far outnumber the positives. In an ideal world, I would love to eliminate all negatives and have athletes only express positives. But this is the real world and any athlete who cares about their sport is going to feel and express anger, frustration, and helplessness occasionally.

In dealing with this reality, you should learn to *balance the scales.* If you're going to be negative when you make mistakes and perform poorly, you should also be positive when you perform well. The immediate goal is to increase the positives. This means rewarding yourself when you perform well. If you beat yourself up over an error, why shouldn't you pat yourself on the back when you get it right. Pump your fist, slap your leg, say, "yes," when you perform well. It will psych you up and make you feel positive and excited.

Once you've balanced the scales by increasing your positives, your next goal is to tip the scales in the positive direction by reducing the negatives.

Ask why you're so hard on yourself when you perform poorly. The best athletes in the world don't always perform their best. Why shouldn't it be okay for you to have down periods in your performances?

Become aware of your negative self-talk and body language. Do things that counter the negativity. For example, after you make a mistake, instead of dropping your head, shrugging your shoulders and saying, "I stink," try bouncing up and down, pumping your fist, and saying, "Come on!"

This step of tipping the scales toward positives is so important because of some recent research that found that negative experiences such as negative self-talk, negative body language, and negative emotions carry more weight than positive experiences. In fact, it takes 12 positive experiences to equal one negative experience. What this means is that for every negative expression you make, whether saying something negative or screaming in frustration, you must express yourself positively 12 times to counteract that one negative expression.

Remember, your self-talk, how you walk, and your body language are skills. If your scale is tipped heavily to the negative side, you have become very skilled at these negative expressions. Like changing any skill, to get rid of these bad ones, you have to identify better skills, make a commitment to changing them, and practice the positive skills until they're ingrained and automatic.

Thought-stopping. As a well-known psychologist once said, "We become what we think of most of the time." If you're always thinking negatively, then you will likely fail. Another useful technique to reduce your negative thinking and develop your positive thinking is called thought-stopping. This strategy involves replacing your negative self-talk with positive self-talk. Using the Thought Stopping Exercise (see page 55), list the negative statements you commonly say to yourself when you're practicing and competing. Next, indicate where and in what situations you say the negative things. This will help you become aware of the situations in which you're most likely to be negative. Then, list positive statements with which you can replace them. For example, after a bad day, you might say "I had a horrible competition." Instead, replace that negative statement with something more positive such as "I'll work hard and do better in the next time."

The thought-stopping sequence goes as follows. When you start to think or say something negative; say "stop" or "positive," then replace it with a positive statement. As you learn this new skill, you'll become aware of yourself saying negative things before you actually say them and you'll automatically say something positive.

THOUGHT-STOPPING EXERCISE

Directions: In the space below, list common negative thoughts that you have, where and when they occur, and positive statements to place them.

Negative Thoughts	Time, Place Situation	Positive Replacement
1.		
2.		
3.		
4.		
5.		
6.		
7.		
8.		

Athlete's Litany. The Athlete's Litany is a group of self-statements used to teach positive thinking and increase confidence (see page 57). The litany is like a practice drill in which you're focusing on ingraining good technical skills. The litany provides the necessary repetition to instill positive thinking skills.

As I've indicated before, athletes are often their own worst enemy. They have a considerable amount of negative thinking and negative self-talk, and this negativity becomes a bad habit. The more athletes say negative things, the better they become at being negative. The litany retrains the bad habit of negativity into a good skill of positive thinking. As with any kind of habit, the only way to correct negative thinking is to practice being positive over and over and over again.

A comment I often get from athletes when they start using the litany is that they don't believe what they're saying. This is just like the practice drill in which they're making a technical correction. In a sense, their muscles don't "believe" the new skill either. In time, though, the new skill is learned and their muscles come to "believe" it. The same holds true for the positive self-statements. By repeating the litany enough times, athletes will start believing it. Just like the improved technique, when they get into a competitive situation, the new skill of positive thinking will emerge and it will improve their performances.

The important thing about the Athlete's Litany is not only to say it, but to say it like you mean it. For example, I could say "I love to compete, I'm a great athlete," but I may not sound very convincing. If I say it like I mean it, then I'm more likely to start believing what I'm saying. Saying the litany with conviction also generates positive emotions and physical feelings that will reinforce its positive message.

A great thing about the Athlete's Litany is that you can personalize it to your needs. Create your own litany of positive self-statements that means something to you. Then, say the litany out loud every morning and every night. Also, say the litany before you train and compete.

ATHLETE'S LITANY

Directions: Repeat the litany when you wake up in the morning, before practice and competitions, before you go to sleep at night, or whenever you have doubts or lose confidence in yourself. Remember to say the litany out loud like you mean it. Also, personalize the litany by adding positive statements that are important to you.

I LOVE SPORTS.

I AM COMMITTED TO BECOMING THE BEST ATHLETE I CAN BE.

I THINK AND TALK POSITIVELY.

I GIVE 100% FOCUS AND INTENSITY WHEN I PRACTICE AND COMPETE.

I AM MY BEST ALLY WHEN I COMPETE.

IF I FOCUS ON PERFORMING MY BEST RATHER THAN ON WINNING OR LOSING, I WILL SUCCEED.

I STRIVE TO PERFORM MY BEST WHEN THE PRESSURE IS ON.

I TRY MY HARDEST REGARDLESS OF WHETHER I AM AHEAD OR BEHIND.

IF I GIVE MY BEST EFFORT, I AM A WINNER.

Keywords. Another useful way to develop your confidence is to use keywords which remind you to be positive and confident. Make a list of words that make you feel positive and good. Then, write them on your equipment where they're visible during practice and competitions. Also, put keywords in noticeable places where you live such as in your bedroom, on your refrigerator door, or in your locker. When you look at a keyword, say it to yourself. Just like the Athlete's Litany, every time you see it, it will sink in further until you truly believe it.

Using negative thinking positively. Even though I very much emphasize being positive at all times, the fact is, you can't always be positive. You don't always perform as well as you want and there is going to be some negative thinking. This awareness was brought home to me by a group of highly-ranked junior athletes I worked with not long ago. During the training camp, I was constantly emphasizing being positive and not being negative. One night at dinner, several of the athletes came up to me and said that sometimes things do just stink and you can't be positive. I realized that negative thinking is normal when you don't perform well and some negative thinking is healthy. It means you care about performing poorly and want to perform better. Negative thinking can be motivating as well because it's no fun to perform poorly and lose. I got to thinking about how athletes could use negative thinking in a positive way. I came up with an important distinction that will determine whether negative thinking helps or hurts performance.

There are two types of negative thinking: give-up negative thinking and fire-up negative thinking. Give-up negative thinking involves feelings of loss and despair and helplessness, for example, "It's over. I can't win this." You dwell on past mistakes and failures. It lowers your motivation and confidence, and it takes your focus away from performing your best. Your intensity also drops because basically you're surrendering and accepting defeat. There is never a place in sports for give-up negative thinking.

In contrast, fire-up negative thinking involves feelings of anger and energy, of being psyched up, for example, "I'm doing so badly. I hate performing this way" (said with anger and intensity). You look to doing better in the future because you hate performing poorly and losing. Fire-up negative thinking increases your motivation to fight and turn things around. Your intensity goes up and you're bursting with energy. Your focus is on attacking and defeating your opponent.

Fire-up negative thinking can be a positive way to turn your performance around. If you're going to be negative, make sure you use fire-up negative thinking. Don't use it too much though. Negative thinking and negative emotions require a lot of energy and that energy should be put in a more positive direction for your training and competitions. Also, it doesn't feel very good to be angry all of the time.

> *"You tell your mind what to do and if you're able to fuel your mind with positive thoughts and confidence, you'll achieve amazing things."*
>
> **1984 Olympic marathon champion Joan Benoit-Samuelson**

CONFIDENCE CHALLENGE

The real test of confidence is how you respond when things are not going your way. I call this the Confidence Challenge. It's easy to stay confident when you're performing well, when the conditions are ideal, and when you're competing against someone whom you're better than. But as I said earlier, an inevitable part of sports is that you'll have some down periods. What separates the best from the rest is that the best athletes are able to maintain their confidence when they're not at the top of their games. By staying confident, they continue to work hard rather than give up because they know that, in time, their performance will come around.

Most athletes when they perform poorly lose their confidence and get caught in the vicious cycle of low confidence and performance. Once they slip into that downward spiral, they rarely can get out of it. In contrast, athletes with prime confidence maintain their confidence and seek out ways to return to their previous level. All athletes will go through periods where they don't perform well. The skill is not getting caught in the vicious cycle and being able to get out of the down periods quickly.

The Confidence Challenge can be thought of as a Prime Sport skill that can be developed. Learning to respond positively to the Confidence Challenge comes from exposing yourself to demanding situations, difficult conditions, and tough opponents in training and competition and practicing positive responses.

There are several key aspects of mastering the Confidence Challenge. First, you need to develop the attitude that demanding situations are challenges to be sought out rather than threats to be avoided. When you're faced with a Confidence Challenge you must see it as an opportunity to become a better athlete. You also need to believe that experiencing challenges is a necessary part of becoming the best athlete you can be. You have to realize that, at first, these challenges are going to be uncomfortable because they are difficult and unfamiliar. As you expose yourself to more challenges, they will become less threatening and more comfortable.

With this perspective, you should seek out every possible challenge in training and competition. Be sure you're well-prepared to meet the challenges. You can't master the Confidence Challenge if you don't have the preparation and skills to do so. Stay positive and motivated in the face of the difficulties. Don't allow yourself to be sucked into the vicious cycle. Then, focus on what you need to do to overcome the challenge rather than on how difficult it may be or how you may fail. Also, accept that you'll make mistakes and may not fully succeed when faced with a challenge for the first time. Don't take this as a failure, but rather as an experience you can learn from to improve next time. Finally, and most importantly, never, ever give up!

"Confidence is the difference in a decisive set."

Chris Evert

CHAPTER FOUR

INTENSITY

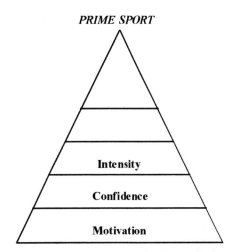

PRIME SPORT

Intensity may be the most important contributor to performance once the competition begins. It's so important because all of the motivation, confidence, focus, and emotions in the world won't help you if your body is not physiologically capable of doing what it needs to do in order for you to perform your best.

Simply put, intensity is the amount of physiological activity you experience in your body including heart rate, respiration, and adrenaline. Intensity is a continuum that ranges from sleep (very relaxed) to terror (very anxious). Somewhere in between those two extremes is the level of intensity at which you perform your best.

Intensity is made up of two components. First, there is the physical experience of intensity, that is, what you actually feel in your body when you are competing. Are you calm or filled with energy? Are you relaxed or tense? Second, there is your perception of the intensity. In other words, do you perceive the intensity positively or negatively? Two athletes can feel the exact same thing physiologically, but interpret those physical feelings in very different ways. One may view the intensity as excitement and it will help his performance. Another may see the intensity as anxiety and it will hurt his performance.

The physical experience and the perception of intensity are affected by several mental factors. If you are not confident, feeling frustrated and angry, and focusing on winning rather than on performing your best, you will see the intensity as negative. In contrast, if you are confident and positive, happy and excited, and focused on performing well, the intensity will be perceived as positive.

> *"It's all about intensity. If you lose it, even just for a little while, you're in trouble."*
>
> **Former NBA player Doc Rivers**

SIGNS OF OVER-AND UNDER-INTENSITY

Intensity produces a wide variety of physical and mental symptoms that can help you recognize when your intensity is too high or too low. By being aware of these signs, you will be able to know when you're not performing at prime intensity and can take steps to reach that ideal level.

Overintensity. Muscle tension and breathing difficulties are the most common signs of overintensity. Most athletes indicate that when they're too intense, they feel tension in their shoulders and their legs, which happen to be the two most important physical areas for many sports. If a swimmer's shoulders are tense, the motion of her strokes will shorten and she won't be able to swim with ease or power. When a high jumper's legs are tense, he loses the ability to run and jump with smoothness and explosiveness.

Many athletes also report that their breathing becomes short and choppy when they get nervous. This restriction in breathing means that they're not getting enough oxygen into their system so they will tire quickly. I've also found that the smoothness of athletes' movement tends to mirror their breathing. If their breathing is long and smooth, so is their movement. If their breathing is abrupt and choppy, their movement is jerky and uncomfortable.

Athletes who are overly intense often exhibit poor posture and a stiff gait. Muscle tension causes their shoulders to rise and their body to seem to close up. Athletes make more mistakes when they're overly intense because anxiety disrupts coordination. Overintensity interferes with motor control that affects technical skills and movement. Athletes who are anxious also increase the pace of the competition. For example, a cyclist goes out too fast early in a road race. Athletes often look rushed and frantic. If opponents are taking their time, overly intense athletes become impatient at the slow pace.

Overintensity negatively influences athletes mentally as well. Anxiety lowers confidence and causes doubts in ability. The physical and mental discomfort produces negative emotions such as frustration, anger, and depression. The anxiety, doubts, and negative emotions hurt focus by drawing athletes' attention away from performing their best and onto how badly they feel.

Underintensity. Though not as common, athletes can also experience underintensity during competition. The most common symptom of underintensity is low energy and lethargy. Athletes lack the adrenaline they need to give their best effort. Though not as discomforting as overintensity, underintensity hurts performance equally because athletes lack the physical requisites such as strength, stamina, and agility to meet the demands of their sport.

Mentally, underintensity undermines motivation. Athletes just don't feel like being out there. The lack of interest caused by too low intensity also impairs their focus because they're easily distracted and have difficulty staying focused on their performances.

"I can't press, I can't get too tight, because then there's a danger that I'll try so hard to do well that I'll mess up."

Former NFL great Marcus Allen

LINE BETWEEN INTENSITY AND TENSITY

The ultimate goal of prime intensity is to find the precise line between intensity and tensity. The closer athletes can get to that line, the more their bodies will work for them in achieving Prime Sport. If athletes cross the line to tensity, their bodies will no longer be physically capable of attaining Prime Sport. Great athletes have the ability to do two things related to this line. First, they have a better understanding of where that line is, so they can "tightrope walk" on it, thereby maximizing what their bodies can give them. Second, they're able to stay on that line longer than other athletes, which enables them to perform at a consistently higher level for longer periods of time.

"I love to hit when the pressure's on. I enjoy the excitement. I try harder. I concentrate more."

Former baseball great Reggie Jackson

PRIME INTENSITY

Prime intensity is the ideal amount of physiological activity necessary for athletes to perform their best. It is also the level of intensity that athletes perceive as most positive and beneficial to their sports performances. Unfortunately, there is no one ideal level of intensity for every athlete. Prime intensity is individual; it's different for everyone. Some athletes perform best relaxed. Others perform best energized, but not too psyched up. Still others perform best unbelievably intense and fired up. Athletes must find out the level of intensity that enables them to perform their best.

You have several goals in developing prime intensity. First, to learn what is your prime intensity. Then, to recognize the signs of overintensity and underintensity. Next, to identify competitive situations in which your intensity may go up or down. Finally, to take active steps to reach and maintain prime intensity throughout a competition.

Your intensity is much like the thermostat maintaining the most comfortable temperature in your house. You always notice when your house is too warm or too cold because you're sensitive to changes in temperature. When the temperature becomes uncomfortable, you adjust the thermostat to a more comfortable level. You can think of your intensity as your internal temperature that needs to be adjusted periodically. You need to be sensitive to when your intensity is no longer comfortable, in other words, it's not allowing you to perform your best. You can then use the intensity control techniques I'll be describing to you to raise or lower your intensity to its prime level.

> *"Intensity has always been the strongest part of my game."*
>
> **Jim Courier**

DETERMINING PRIME INTENSITY

Using the Intensity Identification form (see page 68), you can identify what is your prime intensity. First, think back to several competitions in which you performed very well. Recall your level of intensity. Were you relaxed, energized, or really fired up? Then remember the thoughts, emotions, and physical feelings you experienced during these competitions. Were you positive or negative, happy or angry, relaxed or tense? Second, think back to several competitions in which you performed poorly. Recall your level of intensity. Remember the thoughts, emotions, and physical feelings you had in these competitions. If you're like most athletes, a distinct pattern will emerge. When you perform well, you have a particular level of intensity. This is your prime intensity. There are also common thoughts, emotions, and physical feelings associated with performing well. In contrast, when you're performing poorly, there is a very different level of intensity, either higher or lower than your prime intensity. There are also decidedly different thoughts, emotions, and physical feelings.

Another useful way to help you understand your prime intensity is to experiment with different levels of intensity in practice and see how the differing intensity impacts your performance. Here is a good exercise you can use to learn more about your prime intensity:

Let's say you're working on a drill to improve some aspect of your performance. Break up the drill into three segments. The first segment will emphasize low intensity. Before you begin the drill, take several slow, deep breaths, relax your muscles, and focus on calming thoughts (e.g., "Easy does it," "Cool and calm."). As you start the drill, stay focused on keeping your body relaxed and calm.

The second segment will focus on moderate intensity. Before the drill, take a few deep, but stronger breaths, walk around a bit, and focus on more energetic thoughts (e.g., "Let's go," "Pick it up."). Before the drill, bounce on your feet lightly and feel your intensity picking up. During the drill, pay attention to feeling the intensity and energy in your body and keeping your body moving.

The final segment will highlight high intensity. Before the drill, take several deep, forced breaths with special emphasis on a hard and aggressive exhale, start bouncing up and down immediately, and repeat intense thoughts (e.g., "Fire it up," "Get after it."), saying these out loud with energy and force. Feel the high level of intensity and energy as you begin the drill, and focus on maintaining the intensity with constant movement and high-energy self-talk.

I encourage you to use this exercise for several days so you can see clearly how your intensity impacts your performance. As with the Intensity Identification form, you will probably see a pattern emerge in which you move and perform better at one of the three levels of intensity.

With this knowledge, you will have a good sense of your prime intensity and can then use that information to recognize when you're not at prime intensity and when you need to adjust your intensity to a prime level.

INTENSITY IDENTIFICATION

Directions: In the space below, indicate the mental and physical factors that are related to your   best (prime intensity) and worst (overintensity or underintensity) competitions. At the bottom, summarize the positive and negative factors that distinguish your prime from poor intensity.

	Best Competitions	**Worst Competitions**
Importance of competition		
Difficulty of opponent		
Competitive conditions		
Thoughts		
Emotions		
Physical feelings		

PSYCH-DOWN TECHNIQUES

When you're in a pressure situation during a competition, it's natural for your intensity to go up and for you to feel nervous. If you want to perform your best, you have to take active steps to get your intensity back to its prime level. There are several simple techniques you can use to help you get your intensity back under control.

Deep breathing. When athletes experience overintensity, one of the first things that's disrupted is their breathing. It becomes short and choppy and they don't get the oxygen their body needs to perform its best. The most basic way to lower their intensity then is to take control of their breathing again by focusing on taking slow, deep breaths.

Deep breathing has several important benefits. It ensures that you get enough oxygen so your body can function well. By getting more oxygen into your body, you will relax, feel better, and it will give you a greater sense of control. This increased comfort will give you more confidence and enable you to more easily combat negative thoughts. It will also help you let go of negative emotions such as frustration and anger, and allow you to regain positive emotions such as excitement. Focusing on your breathing also acts to take your mind off of things that may be interfering with your performance and back onto things that will enable you to perform better.

For athletes who participate in sports that involved a series of short performances, such as baseball, football, tennis, and golf, deep breathing should be a part of your between-performance routine (to be discussed further in Chapter Eight). One place in particular where deep breathing can be especially valuable to reduce intensity is before you begin another performance. If you take two deep breaths at this point, you ensure that your body is relaxed and comfortable, and you're focused on something that will help you perform your best.

Muscle relaxation. The most common sign of overintensity is muscle tension. This is the most crippling physical symptom because if your muscles are tight and stiff, you won't be able to perform at your highest level. There are two muscle relaxation techniques, passive relaxation and active relaxation, you can use away from your sport or, in a shortened form, during competitions between performances. Similar to deep breathing, muscle relaxation is beneficial because it allows you to regain control of your body and to make you feel more comfortable physically. It also offers the same mental and emotional advantages as does deep breathing.

Passive relaxation involves imagining that tension is a liquid that fills your muscles creating discomfort that interferes with your body performing its best. By imagining that you have drain plugs on the bottom of your feet, the tension can drain out of your body and you can attain a desired state of relaxation.

To prepare for passive relaxation, lie down in a comfortable position in a quiet place where you won't be disturbed. Use the passive relaxation procedure described on page 72. You can memorize the procedure, have someone guide you through it, or record it on an audiotape and listen to it on your own. As you go through the passive relaxation procedure, take your time, focus on your breathing and your muscles, feel the tension leave your body, and, at the end, focus on your overall state of mental calmness and physical relaxation.

Active relaxation is used when your body is very tense and you can't relax your muscles with passive relaxation. When your intensity is too high and your muscles are tight, it's difficult to just relax them. So instead of trying to relax your muscles, do just the opposite. Tighten them more, then release them. Our muscles work on what is called an opponent principle process. For example, before a competition, your muscle tension might be at an 8, where 1 is totally relaxed and 10 is very tense, but you perform best at a 4. By further tightening your muscles up to a 10 , the natural reaction is for your muscles to rebound back past 8 toward a more relaxed 4. So, making your muscles more tense actually causes them to become more relaxed.

Active relaxation typically involves tightening and relaxing four major muscle groups: face and neck, arms and shoulders, chest and back, and buttocks and legs. It can also be individualized to focus on particular muscles that trouble you the most.

To get ready for active relaxation follow the same preparations as I described for passive relaxation, Use the active relaxation procedure described on page 73. The most important part of active relaxation is learning to tell the difference between states of tension and relaxation. As you go through the active relaxation procedure, focus on the differences between tension and relaxation, be aware of how you are able to induce a greater feeling of relaxation, and, at the end, focus on your overall state of mental calmness and physical relaxation.

These two relaxation procedures can also be used during a competition (for those sports comprised of a series of short performances) in an abbreviated form. Between performances, you can stop for five seconds and allow the tension to drain out of tense parts of your body. Just before the next performance, you can do a set of active relaxation on your shoulders.

PASSIVE RELAXATION

Imagine there are drain plugs on the bottom of your feet. When you open them, all the tension will drain out of your body and you will become very, very relaxed. Take a slow, deep breath.

Now, undo those plugs. Feel the tension begin to drain out of your body. Down from the top of your head, past your forehead, your face and neck; you're becoming more and more relaxed. The tension drains out of your jaw and down past your neck. Now your face and your neck are warm and relaxed and comfortable. Take a slow, deep breath.

The tension continues to drain out of your upper body, past your hands and forearms, and out of your upper arms and shoulders. Now your hands, arms and shoulders are warm and relaxed and comfortable. Take a slow, deep breath.

The tension continues to drain out of your upper body, past your chest and upper back, down past your stomach and lower back, and your upper body is becoming more and more relaxed. There is no more tension left in your upper body. Now your entire upper body is warm and relaxed and comfortable. Take a slow, deep breath.

The tension continues to drain out of your lower body, past your buttocks and down past your thighs, and your knees. Your lower body is becoming more and more relaxed. The tension drains out of your calves. There is almost no more tension left in your body and the last bit of tension drains past your ankles, the balls of your feet, and your toes. Now do a brief survey of your body from head to toe to ensure that there is no more tension left in your body. Your entire body is warm and relaxed and comfortable. Now replace the plugs so that no tension can get back in. Take a slow, deep breath. Feel the calm and relaxation envelop you. Enjoy that feeling and remember what it feels like to be completely relaxed.

ACTIVE RELAXATION

When I say tight, I want you to tighten that body part for five seconds; when I say loose, I want you to relax it.

First, your buttocks and legs. Tight...loose. Feel the relaxation. Take a slow, deep breath. Once again with the buttocks and legs. Tight...loose. The muscles in your buttocks and legs are warm and relaxed. Feel the difference between the states of tension and relaxation in your buttocks and legs. Take a slow, deep breath.

Now your chest and back. Tight...loose. Feel the relaxation. Take a slow, deep breath. Once again with the chest and back. Tight...loose. The muscles in your chest and back are warm and relaxed. Feel the difference between the states of tension and relaxation in your chest and back. Take a slow, deep breath.

Now your arms and shoulders. Tight...loose. Feel the relaxation. Take a slow, deep breath. Once again with the arms and shoulders. Tight...loose. The muscles in your arms and shoulders are warm and relaxed. Feel the difference between the states of tension and relaxation in your arms and shoulders. Take a slow, deep breath.

Now your face and neck. Tight...loose. Feel the relaxation. Take a slow, deep breath. Once again with the face and neck. Tight...loose. The muscles in your face and neck are warm and relaxed. Feel the difference between the states of tension and relaxation in your face and neck. Take a slow, deep breath.

Now every muscle in your body. Be sure that every muscle is as tight as you can get it. Tight...loose. Feel the relaxation. Take a slow, deep breath. Once again with your entire body. Tight...loose. Every muscle in your body is warm and relaxed. Feel the difference between the states of tension and relaxation in your entire body. Take a slow, deep breath.

Now do a mental check list to make sure that every muscle is relaxed. Your feet are relaxed, calves, thighs, buttocks, stomach, back, chest, arms, shoulders, neck, and face. Every muscle in your body is completely relaxed.

Slow pace of competition. A common side effect of overintensity is that athletes tend to speed up the tempo of competition. Athletes in sports such as tennis, golf, baseball, football, and track and field rush between performances almost as if they want to get the competition over with as soon as possible. So, to lower your intensity, slow your pace between performances. Simply slowing your pace and giving yourself time to slow your breathing and relax your muscles will help you lower your intensity to its prime level.

Process focus. One of the primary causes of overintensity is focusing on the outcome of the competition. If you're worried about whether you will win or lose, you're bound to get nervous. The prospect of losing is threatening, so that will make you anxious. The thought of winning, especially if it's against an opponent you have never defeated before, can also be anxiety provoking because it may be unfamiliar or unexpected to you.

To reduce the anxiety caused by an outcome focus, redirect your focus onto the process. Ask yourself, what do I need to do to perform my best? This process focus can include paying attention to your technique or tactics. Or it might involve focusing on mental skills such as positive thinking or the psych-down strategies I am currently describing. You can also shift your focus onto your breathing which will take your mind off of the outcome and will directly relax your body by providing more oxygen to your system.

A process focus takes your mind off things that cause your over-intensity and shifts your focus onto things that will reduce your anxiety, build your confidence, and give you a greater sense of control over your sport (to be discussed further in Chapter Five).

Keywords. Another focusing technique for lowering your intensity is to use what I call intensity keywords. These words act as reminders of what you need to do with your intensity to perform your best (see Intensity Keywords on page 76). Keywords are especially important in the heat of a tight competition when you can get so wrapped up in the pressure that you forget to do the things you need to do in order to perform your best.

By saying the keyword between performances, you'll be reminded to use the psych-down techniques when your intensity starts to go up. I also recommend that you write one or two keywords on a piece of tape which you then put on a piece of your equipment. Looking at the equipment acts as a further reminder to follow the keyword and lower your intensity.

INTENSITY KEYWORDS

Directions: A variety of intensity keywords have been provided below. In the space at the bottom, identify other intensity keywords that you can use.

Psych-Down	Psych-Up
Breathe	Go For It
Loose	Charge
Relax	Attack
Calm	Positive
Easy	Hustle
Trust	Commit

Music. Music is one of the most common tools athletes in many sports use to control their intensity. We all know that music has a profound physical and emotional impact on us. Music has the ability to make us happy, sad, inspired, and motivated. Music can also excite or relax us. Many world-class and professional athletes listen to music before they compete to help them reach their prime intensity.

Music is beneficial in several ways. It has a direct effect on you physically. Calming music slows your breathing and relaxes your muscles. Simply put, it makes you feel good. Mentally, it makes you feel positive and motivated. It also generates positive emotions such as joy and contentment. Finally, calming music takes your mind off aspects of the competition that may cause doubt or anxiety. The overall sensation of listening to relaxing music is a generalized sense of peace and well-being.

Smile. The last technique for lowering intensity is one of the strangest and most effective I've ever come across. A few years ago, I was working with a young professional athlete who was having a terrible practice session. She was performing very poorly and her coach was getting frustrated with her. She approached me during a break feeling angry and depressed, and her body was in knots. She asked me what she could do. I didn't have a good answer until an idea just popped into my head. I told her to smile. She said, I don't want to smile. I told her to smile. She said she was not happy and didn't want to smile. I told her again to smile. This time, just to get me off her back, she did smile. I told her to hold the smile. During the next two minutes there was an amazing transformation. As she stood there with the smile on her face, the tension began to drain out of her body. Her breathing became slow and deep. She said that she was feeling better. In a short time, she was looking more relaxed and happier. She returned to practice, her performance improved, and she made some progress during the remainder of the practice session.

Her response was so dramatic that I wanted to learn how such a change could occur. When I returned to my office, I looked at the research related to smiling and learned two things. First, as we grow up, we become conditioned to the positive effects of smiling. In other words, we learn that when we smile, it means we're happy and life is good. Second, there's been some fascinating research looking at the effects of smiling on our brain chemistry. What this research has found is that when we smile, it releases brain chemicals called endorphines which have an actual physiologically relaxing effect.

> *"I learned a long time ago that one way to maximize potential for performance is to be calm in my mind and body."*
>
> **Former NFL quarterback Brian Sipe**

PSYCH-UP TECHNIQUES

Though less common, letdowns in intensity can also cause your level of performance to decline. A decrease in intensity causes all the things that enable you to perform well to disappear. Physically, you no longer have the blood flow, oxygen, and adrenaline necessary for the strength, agility, and stamina you need to perform your best. Mentally, you lose the motivation and focus that enables you to perform well. Just like psych-down techniques when your intensity is too high, you can use psych-up techniques to raise your intensity when it drops.

Intense breathing. Just as deep breathing can reduce intensity, intense breathing can increase it. If you find your intensity dropping, several hard exhales can take your body and your mind to a more intense level. It's a useful practice before a performance to take two intense breaths. In fact, I encourage you to make intense breathing a part of your competitive routine when you're intensity goes down (to be discussed further in Chapter Eight).

Move your body. Remember that intensity is, most basically, physiological activity. The most direct way to increase intensity is with physical action. In other words, move. Walk or run around, jump up and down. Anything to get your heart pumping and your body going.

High-energy self-talk. One of the main causes of drops in intensity is letdown thoughts. Thinking to yourself, "I've got this won," "The game is over," or "I can't win this," will all result in your intensity decreasing. When this happens, you can be sure your performance will decline. When you start to have these thoughts, you need to replace them with high-energy self-talk. Self-talk such as "Keep attacking," "Close it out," and "Stay pumped" will keep you motivated and focused, and your body will respond with more intensity.

Intensity keywords. Just as you can use keywords to lower intensity, they can also be used to counter letdowns and to psych yourself up (see Intensity Keywords on page 76). Saying intensity keywords such as "Charge" and "Hustle" with conviction and energy will raise your intensity and generate positive thoughts and emotions that will enable you to perform your best.

High-energy body language. It's difficult using high-energy self-talk and intensity keywords without also having high-energy body language. Pumping your fist or slapping your thigh will also get you fired up and will increase your intensity.

Music. The value of music has already been described above. Music can also be used to raise your intensity and get you psyched up and motivated. The overall sensation of listening to high-energy music is a generalized sense of excitement and energy.

> *"I like to fire up, to feel the adrenaline flowing; that's when I perform my best."*
>
> **Chris Evert**

KEY COMPETITIVE SITUATIONS

There are common competitive situations in which you can expect that your intensity will shift away from prime intensity. If you can identify these situations when they occur, you can more quickly take steps to prevent a change in intensity that may hurt your performance. These competitive situations usually relate to when you're either ahead or behind in a competition, or the competition is on the line.

Overintensity is most common in pressure situations such as in the finals of competitions or an overtime period. Anytime you believe that you must win a point or a game, your intensity will probably rise beyond your prime intensity. Underintensity is seen most often in competitive situations where you believe that you have the competition won, for example, you have a big lead or time is running out.

There is not, however, a consistent pattern in how intensity will change for all athletes. Athletes in the same competitive situation can experience different changes in intensity. For example, one athlete may have an increase in intensity and feel very nervous because she's never defeated her opponent before and doesn't totally believe that she can. While another athlete in the same situation might have a decrease in intensity and feel a letdown because she's already mentally in the locker room thinking about her next competition. You have to figure out how you typically react and then use the psych-up and psych-down techniques to achieve and maintain prime intensity.

> *"All pressure is self-inflicted. It's what you make of it, how you let it rub off on you."*
>
> **Olympic track & field champion Sebastian Coe**

CHAPTER FIVE

FOCUS

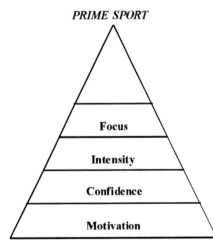

PRIME SPORT

- Focus
- Intensity
- Confidence
- Motivation

Focus is the most misunderstood mental factor among athletes. Most athletes think of focus as concentrating on one thing for a long time. In fact, a number of years ago, former Australian Open tennis champion Hana Mandlikova said that she improved her game by staring at a tennis ball for ten minutes a day. But focusing in most sports is much more complex than that.

Let me introduce a term, attentional field, and then I'll define focus for you. Attentional field is everything inside of you, such as thoughts, emotions, and physical responses, and everything outside of you, including sights and sounds, on which you could focus. Focus is the ability to attend to internal and external cues in your attentional field.

Prime focus involves focusing only on performance-relevant cues in your attentional field. In other words, only focusing on cues that help you to perform your best. Depending on the sport, performance-relevant cues can include technique, tactics, your opponent, the score, time remaining, and many other cues. Prime focus gives you the ability to adjust your focus internally and externally as needed during the course of a competition.

For example, a football quarterback first focuses internally to select the best play based on the current game situation. As the huddle breaks and he moves over center, he widens his focus externally to survey the defensive alignment. When the ball is hiked and he drops back to pass, the quarterback focuses on the routes of his receivers until he finds one who is open, at which time he narrows his focus onto that receiver and throws him the football.

Poor focus involves focusing on performance-irrelevant cues in your attentional field. That is, focusing on cues that will hurt your performance. There are two types of harmful cues. Interfering cues are those that will directly hurt your performance such as negative thoughts, anxiety, and concern over who your next opponent will be if you win. Irrelevant cues are those that simply distract you from an effective focus including what you'll have for dinner tonight or the project that you must finish by tomorrow.

> *"My concentration level blocks out everything. Concentration is why some athletes are better than others. You develop that concentration is training. You can't be lackadaisical in training and concentrate in a meet."*
>
> **Olympic 400-meter hurdles champion Edwin Moses**

FOCUS STYLES

One of the most important developments I've made in my work in recent years is in understanding the importance of identifying athletes' focus styles. A focus style is a preference for paying attention to certain cues. Athletes tend to be more comfortable focusing on some cues and avoid or don't pay attention to other cues. Every athlete has a dominant style that impacts all aspects of their sports performance. This dominant style will surface most noticeably when they're under pressure. The two types of focus styles are internal and external.

Internal focus style. Athletes with an internal focus style perform best when they're totally and consistently focused on their sport during a practice session or a competition. They need to keep their focus narrow, thinking only about their sport. These athletes tend to be easily distracted by activity in their immediate surroundings. If they broaden their focus and take their mind off their sport, for example, if they talk about non-sport topics with their coach during a practice, they'll become distracted and will have trouble narrowing their focus back onto their sport.

External focus style. Athletes with an external focus style perform best when they only focus on their sport when they're about to begin a drill in practice or begin a competition. At all other times, they broaden their focus and take their mind off their sport. These athletes have a tendency to think too much and become negative and critical. This overly narrow focus causes them to lose confidence and experience overintensity. For these athletes, it's essential that they take their focus away from their sport when they're not actually performing.

External focus style runs counter to beliefs held by many coaches. They think that if athletes are not totally focused on their sport, then they're not serious about it and they won't perform their best. Yet, for athletes with an external focus style, they don't want to think too much or be too serious because this causes them to be negative and critical. They'll perform their best when they're not thinking too much about their sport and they simply allow their natural abilities to emerge on their own.

> *"The most important thing is focus. You must divorce yourself from what is going on around you."*
>
> **Former NBA great Calvin Murphy**

IDENTIFYING YOUR FOCUS STYLE

With this understanding, you need to identify what is your focus style. Are you an athlete who needs to keep your mind on your sport constantly in order for you to perform well? Or are you someone who thinks too much and needs to keep your mind off your sport until its time to perform?

Recall past competitions and practices when you've performed well. Were you totally focused on your sport or were you keeping your mind off your sport? Also, recall past competitions and practices when you've performed poorly. Were you thinking too much or were you distracted by things going on around you? If you're like most athletes, a pattern will emerge in which you tend to perform best when you focus one way and you perform poorly when you focus another way.

Understanding your focus style is essential for you to be able to manage it effectively. This process involves knowing how you focus best and actively focusing in a way that is consistent with your focus style. This ability to manage your focus style well is most important in pressure situations. There is a tendency for athletes under pressure to revert back to a focus style that will interfere with rather than help their performance. For example, if you're someone who performs best with an external focus style, you may find yourself turning your focus inward when the pressure is on. You may start to think too much and become negative and critical.

When you start to lose your prime focus style under pressure, you must become aware that you're moving away from it and that you need to take steps to redirect your focus back to the style that works best for you. Continuing the previous example, when you realize that you're focusing internally too much, you should actively turn your focus outward by looking around and taking your mind off your sport.

> *"When I'm getting ready for a fight, I like to focus on what I have to do, and talking about it beforehand won't get the job done."*
>
> **Former boxing great Tommy Hearns**

Mag-Lite® Focus

I've developed a useful tool to help you understand your focus style and to develop focus control. A Mag-Lite® is a flashlight whose beam can be adjusted to illuminate a wide area or to brighten a narrow area. Your focus can be thought of as a Mag-Lite® beam you project that illuminates on what you want to focus.

Athletes with an internal focus style want to keep their Mag-Lite® beam narrow at all times, only illuminating sport-related things during practice or competitions. If you have an internal focus style, your goal is to stay focused on necessary training or competitive cues and to block out unnecessary external distractions. To accomplish this, narrow your Mag-Lite® beam by keeping your eyes within the confines of the practice or competitive setting and avoid talking to others. Focus on important sport cues, for example, the proper technique for the next drill or your intensity for the next performance.

Athletes with an external focus style want to widen their Mag-Lite® beam between drills and performances to take their mind off their sport, then narrow their beam shortly before they begin the next drill or performance. If you have an external focus style, your goal is to direct your focus off your sport between drills in practice and between performances in competitions. To do this, when you're not actually performing, whether in practice or competition, widen your Mag-Lite® beam by looking around you and talking to your coach or other athletes. This will keep you from thinking too much and becoming negative and critical. Shortly before you begin the next drill in practice or next performance in a competition, narrow your Mag-Lite® beam, focusing specifically on something that will help you perform well.

There are also times when, regardless of your focus styles, you'll need to narrow or widen your Mag-Lite® beam in order to adapt to the demands of the competitive situation. For example, a basketball point guard would have to a wide beam as she brings the ball up the court and then she would need to narrow her focus as she decides to pass the ball or take a shot.

"I widened the iris on the camera, stepped back and realized how silly I was being. My focus had gotten way too narrow."

PGA golfer Payne Stewart

FOCUS CONTROL

Developing focus control is essential if you're going to ensure that your focus style helps rather than hurts your sports performance. There are several steps in the focus control process. First, you have to identify your focus style and understand how it impacts your sport. Next, you must recognize internal and external cues that help and hurt your performances. Finally, you have to adjust your focus internally and externally as needed during practice and competitions.

The eyes have it. We obtain most of our information about the world through our eyes. The most direct way to control our Mag-Lite® beams is to control our eyes. You can think of your eyes as Mag-Lite® flashlights that you can adjust wide or narrow. If you want to minimize the external distractions during practice or competitions, narrow your Mag-Lite® beam by keeping your eyes down and on the sport setting, for example, within the confines of the oval track, ice rink, swimming pool, basketball court, or golf course. If you're distracted by something, either look away or turn away from it. If you're not looking at something, it can't distract you.

Conversely, if you find that you're thinking too much or being negative or critical, widen your Mag-Lite® beam by raising your eyes and looking around you. For example, see who's performing nearby. By looking around, you'll be distracted from your thoughts, you'll be able to clear your mind, and then you can narrow your Mag-Lite® beam in preparation for your next performance.

> *"When I'm on the mound, I'm so locked in I don't even see the dugouts. It's just me and the glove. There's no way I can hear what's going on in the bleachers."*

Major League Baseball pitcher Roger Clemens

Outcome vs. process focus. Perhaps the greatest obstacle to prime focus is having an outcome focus during a competition. Outcome focus involves focusing on the possible results of a competition: winning, losing, rankings, or who you might defeat or lose to. I tell athletes that an outcome focus is the kiss of death in sports.

Many athletes believe that by focusing on the outcome, that is, on winning the competition, they're more likely to achieve that outcome. What most athletes don't realize is that having an outcome focus actually hurts performance and makes it less likely that they will win. Every time you shift from a process focus to an outcome focus, your performance will decline. This drop in performance occurs for several reasons. First, you're no longer focusing on things that will help you perform well. Second, it causes your intensity to move away from prime intensity, either up because you start to get nervous over the possibility of losing, or down because you think you already have the competition won.

Athletes don't understand several key things about outcome focus. The outcome comes after the process has occurred and the competition is over. The outcome is totally unrelated to the process of the competition. In fact, the result of an outcome focus is usually the exact opposite of the outcome athletes want, specifically, Prime Sport and winning the competition.

The way to achieve the desired outcome of the competition is to focus on the process of the competition. Process focus involves focusing on aspects of the competition that will enable you to perform your best, for example, technique, tactics, intensity, or emotions. If you perform your best, you're more likely to win.

Focus on what you can control. A major focusing problem I see with many athletes is that they focus on things over which they have no control. Athletes worry about their opponent, the weather, or the conditions, to name a few things outside of athletes' control. This focus has no value because they can't do anything about those things. This kind of focus hurts performance because it lowers confidence and causes worry and anxiety. It also distracts athletes from what they need to focus on. The fact is, there's only one thing that athletes can control, and that is themselves. For example, their attitude, thoughts, emotions, and intensity. If athletes focus on those things, they'll be more confident and relaxed, and they'll be better able to focus on what they need to do in order to perform their best.

Four P's. I have a general rule you can follow that will help you identify what kinds of things you should focus on in your sport. I call it the four P's. The first P is *positive.* You should focus on positive things that will help your performance and avoid negative things that will hurt it. The second P is *process.* As I've just explained, you should focus on what you need to do to perform your best. The third P is *present.* You should focus on what you need to do right now to perform well at this moment. You shouldn't focus on the past because it's out of your control and you can't change it. You also shouldn't focus on the future because it's too far away to do anything about. The only way to control the future is to control the present. The only way to control the present is to focus on it. The last P is *progress.* There's a tendency for many athletes to compare themselves with other athletes, seeing others having better results and getting ahead of them in the rankings. How your opponents perform is outside of your control. What you should focus on is your improvement. Athletes develop at different rates. An athlete who is ahead of you now may not even be in sight behind you in a year. What's important is that you see yourself progressing toward the goals you want to achieve.

"Concentrate on what's happening now, not what happened two plays ago, not what is going to happen in five minutes. Play for the now."

NBA player Bill Wennington

FOCUSING VS. THINKING

A mistake many athletes make is that they equate focusing with thinking. They believe that if they're thinking about, for example, a penalty kick in soccer or a free throw in basketball, then they're also focusing on it and it will help their performance. However, there is a big difference between athletes focusing on their sport and thinking about their sport. This distinction impacts not only athletes' ability to concentrate on important aspects of their sport, but it also affects their motivation, confidence, intensity, and emotions.

Focusing simply involves attending to internal or external cues. This process is impartial, objective, unemotional, and detached from judgment or evaluation. If you make a mistake on something on which you were focusing, you're able to accept it and not be overly disappointed by the failure. In a focusing mode, you're able to use the failure as information to correct the problem and focus better in the future.

In contrast, thinking is connected to your ego-investment in your sport, that is, how important your sport is to you. Thinking is judgmental and critical. If you make a mistake or perform poorly when you're in a thinking mode, it hurts your confidence and causes negative emotions such as frustration and anger. Thinking actually interferes with your ability to focus in a way that will help your performance and it will cause your performances to deteriorate.

"You can't think and hit at the same time."

Baseball legend Yogi Berra

INSIDE THE MIND OF YOUR OPPONENT

When athletes do not have full command of their performances, they must direct most of their focus to the technical, tactical, and mental aspects of their sport with little attention pointed toward their opponent. In other words, they have to perform entirely inside their head.

This phenomenon occurs because athletes have not instilled key skills that would enable them to "get out of their head." Typically, these athletes have not fully ingrained the technical, tactical, and mental aspects of their sport to the point that these skills are fully integrated and automatic. Much of their focus must be on making sure they do the things that will enable them to perform well. For example, a soccer player must focus on her dribbling or a runner must pay attention to his pace. These athletes also lack the confidence in their ability. Without that trust in their performances, they must stay inside their head to ensure that they do the right things.

In contrast, Prime Sport enables athletes to perform "inside the mind of their opponent." This expression means that they're able to project themselves into their opponent and can focus more on their opponent and how they can be defeated.

Performing inside the mind of your opponent means that you have confidence in your ability. You trust that the technical, tactical, and mental skills and habits you have ingrained will emerge automatically and enable you to perform your best. Because of this, you can direct more of your attention to your opponent's performances. You can focus on their strengths and weaknesses, and devise a plan that will enable you to overcome them.

The ability to perform inside the mind of your opponent evolves out of your efforts to achieve Prime Sport. You must first develop the skills and habits that enable you to perform your best. During this process, you must also gain the confidence in your ability. This belief comes from practice and competitive experience. As you have success performing in competition, you will come to trust your ability and allow it to emerge automatically.

With a foundation of skills and confidence, you can then intentionally widen your Mag-Lite® beam and direct your focus toward your opponent. As you're performing, you can ask yourself questions about them: What are their strengths and weaknesses? What strategy can I use to neutralize their strengths and take advantage of their weaknesses? Simply by asking these questions, you're taking the first step to performing inside the mind of your opponent. At first, you will have to do this deliberately. In time, though, this skill will also become automatic and every time you compete, you will naturally perform inside the mind of your opponent.

> *"The bigger it gets, the smaller you've got to think. What you want to think about is what you can do something about. Think about that next play. Put all of your effort into it, and then go on to the next play after that."*
>
> **Virginia Tech football coach Frank Beamer**

CHAPTER SIX

EMOTIONS

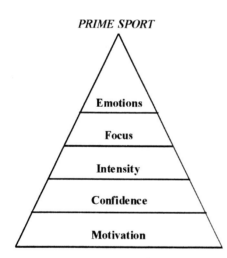

PRIME SPORT

- Emotions
- Focus
- Intensity
- Confidence
- Motivation

At the top of the Prime Sport Pyramid sits emotions. It is closest to the top of the pyramid because emotions will ultimately dictate how you perform throughout a competition. Emotions during a competition can cover the spectrum from excitement and joy to frustration and anger. emotions are often strong and, most troublesome, they can linger and hurt your performances long after you first experience them.

Negative emotions hurt performance both physically and mentally. They first cause athletes to lose their prime intensity. With frustration and anger, their intensity goes up and leads to muscle tension, breathing difficulties, and a loss of coordination. It also saps energy and causes them to tire quickly. When athletes experience despair and helplessness, their intensity drops sharply and they no longer have the physical capabilities to perform well.

Negative emotions also hurt athletes mentally. Fundamentally, negative emotions are a response to the perceived threat that athletes will fail in the situation. Their emotions are telling them that, deep down, they're not confident in their ability to perform well and to win the competition. Their confidence will decline and they will have more negative thoughts to go along with their negative emotions. Also, since negative emotions are so strong, athletes will have difficulty focusing on what will help them to perform well. The negative emotions draw their attention onto all of the negative aspects of their performance. Finally, negative emotions hurt their motivation to perform because it's no longer fun and they just don't feel good.

Emotions come from past experiences in similar situations in the form of beliefs and attitudes athletes hold about performing and competing. The emotions associated with these beliefs and attitudes are commonly known as the "baggage" people carry from their past. Their perceptions from the past impact their present even though the emotions may not be appropriate or useful in the present situation. One of the most difficult aspects of emotions is that they become habits that cause athletes to automatically respond with a certain emotional reaction to a particular circumstance even when that emotional response does more harm than good. Martina Hingis' behavior in the 1999 French Open final against Steffi Graf is an example of such destructive behavior. Her frustration and anger, as expressed by pouting, racquet throwing, and, ultimately, her tanking, led to her losing the match and embarrassing herself.

Negative emotions can be provoked by many occurrences during a competition including bad calls, senseless mistakes, making an error at a crucial point in the competition, and just performing poorly. All of these events share two common elements that lie at the heart of what causes the negative emotions: Athletes feel that the path to a goal is being blocked and they don't seem to have control over removing the obstacle. For example, a boxer is losing to someone and no matter what he tries, he can't seem to turn the bout around. The boxer is likely to experience frustration and anger initially. These emotions can be helpful at first because they motivate him to fight to clear the path to his goal and regain control of the bout. If he's unable to change the course of the fight, then he may experience depression and helplessness, in which he accepts that he can not win, so he just gives up.

LET THE PUNISHMENT FIT THE CRIME

In my work with high-level athletes, I have seen extremely negative emotional reactions to the smallest failures. A missed putt, a few errors in practice, or falling behind early in hockey game, produced frustration and anger that seemed to be out of proportion to the magnitude of the failure. For example, a young gymnast I worked with would beat herself up emotionally for making a mistake in practice. Her level of performance would steadily decline and she would feel terrible about her gymnastics and herself. By the end of the day, she would be battered and bruised by her own emotions. Clearly, the punishment did not fit the crime.

Be sure that your emotions are proportional to what causes them. Ask yourself whether a few mistakes are worth the frustration and anger you might feel and express to yourself. Are you being fair to yourself? When the severity of the punishment exceeds the seriousness of the crime, you have lost perspective on how important your sport is in your life. It might be worth getting frustrated and angry if you didn't get into the college of your choice or you lost your job, but are these strong negative emotions worth feeling over some unimportant mistakes?

You should also consider whether these emotions help or hurt your sports performances. Negative emotions can raise your performance at first because they increase your intensity and get you to fight harder. After a short time though, your performance begins to decline and it usually spirals downward into a vicious cycle from there. Negative emotions actually hurt your performances and keep you from reaching your goals. Why would you allow yourself to experience emotions (frustration, anger, depression) and act in a way (throwing a tantrum, choking, giving up) that ensures failure rather than helps you achieve success?

It's okay to be disappointed when you make mistakes or lose. In fact, you should feel that way. It means that you care about your sport and want to do better. But when your emotions are stronger and more hurtful than they should be given how minor the crime is and how often it occurs (you will make a lot of mistakes during your sports career), then you need to look at why your punishment far exceeds the crime you committed.

Look at the best athletes in the world. Sports are very important to them because it is their life and livelihood. How upset do they get when they perform poorly and lose? Some get very upset. Overall, though, considering how important sports are to them, most great athletes handle mistakes and losses pretty well. In fact, one reason why the best athletes in the world are at the top is because they have the ability to control their emotions rather than their emotions controlling them.

> *"I realized that nobody's perfect. In a way it was such news to me because I'd been in an adult world, and there are such adult expectations to be perfect about everything. And you know, you don't have to be."*
>
> **Monica Seles**

EMOTIONAL THREAT VS. EMOTIONAL CHALLENGE

In recent years, I have found that a simple distinction appears to lie at the heart of the emotional reactions athletes have to their sport: threat vs. challenge. Emotional threat is the perception that winning is all-important and failure is unacceptable. Emotional threat is most often associated with too great an emphasis on winning, results, and rankings. Pressure to win from parents, coaches, and athletes themselves is also common. With these beliefs, it is easy to see why competing in a sport would be emotionally threatening.

Emotional threat manifests itself in a negative "emotional chain" in which each link separately and cumulatively makes athletes feel badly and hurts their performances. The most common reaction to a threat is the desire to avoid the threat. There is often a loss of motivation to perform and compete, especially when the threat of losing is immediate, for example, when an athlete is behind in a competition (think of giving up as a major loss of motivation). Emotional threat also suggests to athletes that they're incapable of overcoming the situation that is causing the threat, so their confidence is hurt and they're overwhelmed with negative and defeatist thoughts. The threat produces strong negative emotions such as fear, anger, frustration, depression, despair, and helplessness.

The emotional threat also causes anxiety and all of the negative physical symptoms associated with overintensity. The previous links in the emotional chain make it nearly impossible to focus effectively because there are so many negative things pulling athletes' focus away from a useful process focus. All of the previous links in the chain ultimately result in very poor performance and little enjoyment in their sport.

In contrast, emotional challenge is associated with athletes enjoying the process of their sport regardless of whether they win or lose. The emphasis is on having fun and seeing the competition as exciting and enriching. Sports, when seen as an emotional challenge, are an experience that is relished and sought out at every opportunity. Thus, emotional challenge is highly motivating, to the point where athletes love being in pressure situations.

Emotional challenge communicates to athletes that they have the ability to meet the demands of their sport, so they're confident and filled with positive thoughts. Emotional challenge generates many positive emotions such as excitement, joy, and satisfaction. It also stimulates athletes' bodies to achieve prime intensity, where their bodies are relaxed, energized, and physically capable of performing their best. Athletes also have the ability to attain prime focus, in which they're totally focused on what enables them to perform their best. All of these links in the emotional challenge chain lead athletes to Prime Sport and great enjoyment in their sport.

"Emotionally it was my best program ever."

Tara Lipinski after winning Olympic gold medal

EMOTIONAL STYLES

I have found four emotional styles among athletes. These styles involve characteristic ways in which athletes respond emotionally to their sport. Athletes with a particular style react in a predictable way any time they find themselves in a threatening situation.

The *seether* feels frustration and anger build slowly during the course of a competition. They appear to be in emotional control, but that is only because the negative emotions haven't surfaced yet. They're able to keep the frustration and anger in check as long as they are performing well and the competition is mostly going their way. If the competition turns or they make a crucial error, they can explode and lose control emotionally. In most cases, they're not able to reestablish control and end up losing the competition.

The *rager* also feels anger and frustration strongly, but it is expressed immediately and openly. For this type of athlete, showing strong emotions acts as a form of relief. The emotions arise, are expressed, and released. By doing this, the rager is able to maintain a kind of emotional equilibrium. Up to a point, this ongoing emotional outlet helps their performance by increasing motivation and intensity. However, though these athletes let the negative emotions out, they do not really let them go. If the competition turns against them, the rage builds until it finally engulfs and controls them. At this point, their emotions become their enemy and their performance deteriorates.

The *brooder* also feels strong emotions, but, unlike the seether and the rager, the most common emotions are despair and helplessness. These athletes tend to dwell on negative experiences, thoughts, and feelings and can be seen as pouting during a competition. Brooders are very sensitive to the highs and lows of a competition and their emotions tend to mirror its course. If they're performing well and winning, they're fine, but if they perform poorly and are losing, the "down" emotions emerge and impact their performance. They possess a strong defeatist attitude and are best known for their giving up in pressure situations. There are no world-class or professional athletes who completely fit this emotional style because someone could not reach such a high level of performance if their dominant emotional style was as a brooder. However, there are many athletes at the highest level who have some brooding qualities.

The *zen master* is the rarest of the emotional styles because they're largely unaffected by threat and negative emotions. As if they're covered in teflon, errors, poor performance, and losing seem to slide right off of them. They have the ability to not let pressure situations affect them and they're able to let go of past mistakes and failure. The zen master rarely shows emotions, either negative or positive, and maintains an consistent demeanor even in the most critical competitive situations.

What emotional style best describes you? Think back to competitions you have performed in that did not go well. How did you respond emotionally? Were you a seether, rager, brooder, or zen master? It's likely that a pattern of emotional reactions will emerge in your sport that place you into one of the four emotional styles.

Emotional styles are not easy to change. In fact, there is some evidence that we are born with a particular temperament and we are "hard-wired" that way. If this is true, then it is difficult to change your emotional style. The goal then is not to alter your basic emotional response to the world, but instead to master your emotional style so that it helps rather than hurts your sports performance.

> *"I don't get real emotional. Whatever happens, good or bad, I have to keep the same attitude."*
>
> **NBA player Mike Bibby**

EMOTIONAL MASTER OR VICTIM

Many athletes believe that they have little control of their emotions and there is nothing they can do to gain control. If their emotions hurt them, they just have to accept it because they can't do anything about it. I call these athletes *emotional victims*, where their emotions have total control over them, they possess unhealthy and unproductive emotional habits, and their emotions interfere with their happiness and their ability to perform well and succeed.

Despite these perceptions, my work has clearly shown that athletes are capable of becoming *emotional masters*. Athletes can gain control of their emotions. They can develop healthy and productive emotional habits. Their emotions can facilitate their happiness and their ability to succeed.

Emotions are a simple, but not easy, choice. They are a simple choice because if athletes have the option to feel badly and perform poorly or feel good and perform well, they will certainly choose the latter option. However, emotions are not an easy choice because past emotional baggage and old emotional habits lead athletes to respond emotionally in the present in ways that are unhealthy and result in poor performance. The choice comes with awareness of when old emotional habits will arise and choosing a positive emotional response that will lead to good feelings and successful performance.

> *"Emotion is what makes me what I am today. It makes me perform bigger than I am."*
>
> **Charles Barkley**

RESPONDING TO FRUSTRATION

Frustration is at the heart of every negative emotional reaction. Frustration, in its most basic form, is the emotional reaction to athletes' efforts toward a goal being thwarted. In other words, if their goal is to perform well and win a competition, then athletes may experience frustration if they're making mistakes, performing poorly, or are behind in a competition.

Frustration can initially be motivating because it pushes athletes to find a way to remove the obstacles to their goal. If they're unable to turn the competition around, then the initial frustration will become more persistent and stronger. Depending on their emotional style, athletes will either begin to experience anger or despair. If further efforts go unrewarded, then the negative emotions will likely take over and athletes will get caught in the negative emotional chain I spoke of earlier.

If athletes can learn to respond positively to frustration when it first occurs, they can prevent other stronger negative emotions from arising and they can stop the negative emotional chain before it starts. Their goal is to react positively to the first indication of negative emotions. This reaction starts with developing a positive attitude about the things that lead to frustration such as errors, poor performance, and losing. It means making a shift from an attitude of emotional threat to one of emotional challenge.

Emotional threat is the primary cause of frustration in response to mistakes. Remember that for athletes who experience emotional threat, failure of any sort is unacceptable. The threat response to frustration causes athletes to dwell on the past. They continue to worry about mistakes and poor performance even though there is nothing they can do about the past. These athletes also perform scared because they're afraid of having to face what they perceive as failure. What they don't realize is that this attitude makes it more likely that they will make mistakes, perform poorly, and lose because they put great pressure on themselves to be perfect. Athletes who perform under emotional threat are also emotional victims who feel helpless to do anything about how they feel and can be expected to perform their worst in important competitive situations.

Yet, failure, in the form of mistakes, poor performance, and losses, is a normal and inevitable part of sport. The best athletes in the world perform poorly and lose competitions. All athletes must accept that they will also perform poorly and they will lose periodically. These "failures" do not make athletes failures. Even if athletes make mistakes and lose, they can still be good athletes who perform well and are successful most of the time. With this emotional challenge attitude, athletes can unburden themselves of the unrealistic pressure that they must perform perfectly and win every time they compete. With this weight off their shoulders, mistakes and losses will no longer be a threat and will be less likely to trigger frustration.

Changing this attitude where failure is unacceptable requires that athletes alter their goal of performance. Most athletes who have an attitude of emotional threat have perfection as their goal. Athletes who strive for perfection will continue to experience frustration and the negative emotional chain because they will never achieve the unrealistic and unattainable goal of perfection.

A healthier and more reasonable goal is *excellence*, which I define as performing well most of the time. The goal of excellence still sets a high standard of performance, but it also allows the possibility and acceptance of mistakes and losses. Consider this: if a baseball player gets a hit one out of three at-bats, he is deemed a star. A gymnast who scores a 9.6 will place highly in a meet. Excellence relieves the pressure of having to be perfect and never make a mistake or perform poorly. Martina Navratilova once told me that early in her career, her perfectionism was the greatest obstacle holding her back. When she made the attitude shift from perfection to excellence her level of play rose dramatically and she became the athlete we saw dominate women's tennis for almost two decades.

With this emotional challenge attitude in place, you're in a position to take practical steps to counter the frustration you will periodically experience. First, you can learn to identify when frustration usually begins for you. Frustration typically occurs in response to a pattern of mistakes or poor performance. Perhaps it is after you have made the same mistake three times or have been beaten by the same opponent twice before. The next step is to recognize a pattern before frustration arises. If you make the same mistake several times in a row, you know that if you repeat the mistake you will become frustrated. It's also important to stay focused on the present rather than dwelling on past mistakes. Having realized that frustration is just around the corner, you can find a solution to the problem so the pattern doesn't continue. For example, make a technical or tactical correction that will enable you to stop making that same mistake.

Also, realize that you have the opportunity to be an emotional master rather than an emotional victim. As an emotional master, you can choose how you will react to how you're performing. Choose to feel badly and perform poorly or opt to feel good and perform better. In fact, how quickly you make the choice in response to frustration will determine how long you continue to perform poorly and whether you ultimately win or lose the competition. The sooner you make the right choice, the sooner you can raise your performance and have a chance to win.

EMOTIONAL MASTERY

The process of emotional mastery begins with recognizing the negative emotional reactions that hurt your sports performances. When you start to feel negative emotions during a competition, be aware of what they are, for instance, frustration, anger, or depression. Then identify what situation caused them.

After the competition, consider what was the underlying cause of the emotions. This might require you to examine your emotional baggage. If the emotions are strong and you find that they present themselves in other parts of your life, you might consider seeking professional help. Such guidance can assist you in better understanding your emotional habits, how they may interfere with many aspects of your life, and how you can learn new emotional responses that will better serve you in your sport and in your life.

To continue the process of emotional mastery in practice and competition, specify alternative emotional reactions to the situations that commonly trigger negative emotions. For example, instead of yelling, "I am terrible," you could slap your thigh and say, "Come on, better next time." This positive emotional response will help you let go of the past mistakes, motivate you to perform better next time, generate positive emotions that will give you more confidence, and allow you to focus on what will help you raise the level of your performance.

Recalling that mental skills like emotional mastery are skills, this positive reaction will not be easy at first because your negative emotional habits are well ingrained. With practice and the realization that you feel better and your performance improves with a positive response, you will, in time, retrain your emotions into a positive emotional habit.

SECTION IV:

PRIME SPORT SKILLS

CHAPTER SEVEN

PRIME SPORT TRAINING

As my first law of preparation indicates, competitions aren't won on the day of the competition, just before the competition, or even during the competition. Rather, they are won in training. What you do in training will determine how you perform and the ultimate outcome of the competition. Training is where the development of Prime Sport begins. It's the place where all of the physical, technical, tactical, and mental requirements of sport are established.

Despite this importance, I'm constantly amazed by the poor quality of training in which I see athletes engage, even at the world-class and professional levels. I see poor effort, ineffective focus, and little intensity. Yet these athletes expect to perform their best in competition. That's unlikely to happen because they're not engaging in prime training. Prime training involves maintaining the highest level of effort, focus, and intensity consistently throughout a practice session. Without prime training, Prime Sport will never be achieved.

> *"Don't mistake activity for training. Practice it the right way."*
>
> **Basketball coaching legend John Wooden**

POSITIVE CHANGE FORMULA

Change of any sort, whether physical, technical, tactical, or mental, doesn't occur automatically. There is a three-step process that will enable you to develop your Prime Sport skills in the quickest and most efficient way possible. I call it the Positive Change Formula (see below). First, you have to become aware of what you're doing incorrectly and how to improve it. Second, you need to control what you want to improve. Finally, you must put in the necessary repetition to ingrain the positive changes fully. Developing your Prime Sport skills involves an awareness of your physical, technical, tactical, and mental states, taking active steps to control them, and doing sufficient repetition to make the changes automatic. This process produces positive change, which leads to Prime Sport.

POSITIVE CHANGE FORMULA

Awareness + Control + Repetition = POSITIVE CHANGE

PRIME SPORT TRAINING

Too often, I see athletes begin training without any clear idea of what they're doing there. They have nothing in particular they're working on and so they aren't working on anything specific to improve. When this happens, athletes are not only not improving, they're also making it more difficult to improve because they're ingraining old and ineffective skills, which makes it harder to learn new skills.

Goal and purpose. To prevent this, you need to always train with a goal and a purpose. A goal is some aspect of your sport that you want to improve. It might be physical, technical, tactical, or mental. A purpose is something specific you work on during practice that will enable you to achieve your goal. For example, if a figure skater's goal is to improve the elevation of her jumps, her purpose might be to do six sets of plyometrics every other day to increase her leg strength and power. Or if a long jumper's goal is to improve his confidence, his purpose might be to use more positive body language between jumps. Every time you go to practice, you should have a goal and a purpose. If you don't, you'll be getting better at getting worse.

100% focus and intensity. Another area most athletes need to work on is their focus and intensity in training. As my fifth law of preparation suggests, athletes want to train at a level of focus and intensity that will allow them to perform their best in competition. Athletes will perform in a competition at the level of focus and intensity at which they train. Ideally, athletes should perform at 100% focus and intensity. As I indicated in Chapters Four and Five, athletes have unique intensity and focus styles in which they perform their best. When I talk about 100% focus and intensity, I mean training at or near the level of focus and intensity that allows athletes to perform their best.

Too often I see athletes training at a level much different than the level at which they want to compete. When they're just practicing, they may be at 70% focus and intensity. In simulated competitions such as scrimmages in basketball or practice matches in tennis, they may up their focus and intensity to 80%. When they get to a competition, they want to perform at 100%. When they try to do this, one of two things happens. Since they've been training at 70 to 80% focus and intensity, that's what comes out in the competition. Or they try to perform at 100% focus and intensity, but since they haven't trained at that level, their performance actually gets worse rather than better. In either case, the result is that they don't perform their best.

Train for adversity. As I suggested in Chapter Three with respect to confidence, an essential skill that you need to develop to perform your best is responding positively to adversity. Most athletes like to train in ideal conditions, but conditions are rarely perfect in competition. Too often in practice, I see athletes put forth less effort or stop completely when the conditions get too difficult. Athletes will say it doesn't matter since it's just practice. But athletes don't realize two things. As my fourth law of preparation states, what you do in practice is what you will do in a competition. If you give up in practice when things get too tough, then you're becoming skilled at giving up in the face of adversity. It is often how athletes respond to adversity that determines who wins the competition. The reality is that difficult conditions occur for all competitors, so your opponent also has to deal with them. What makes the difference in a competition is who responds to the adversity best.

The only way to learn to compete in adverse conditions is to practice in them. This skill comes from accepting that the conditions will interfere with your ability to perform your best and also realizing that your opponent must deal with them as well. Learning to respond positively to adversity comes from realizing that you probably won't perform your best in difficult conditions. You may not realize that you don't have to perform well to win. You only need to perform better than your opponent. By training for adversity, you come to understand the adverse conditions and you learn how to adapt yourself to them. By training for adversity, you develop the skills so that your performance doesn't deteriorate too much due to the tough conditions.

Responding positively to adversity also comes from being determined not to let the adversity beat you. A part of this is the ability to accept that you will make more mistakes and to not allow yourself to become frustrated because your performance declines. You must stay positive and motivated even when things get tough. Having trained for adversity, when you compete in adverse conditions, you can say, "I've been training in these conditions. I know what to do to perform well. This is no big deal."

One more thing, one more time. One of the greatest lessons I have learned from world-class athletes came from 1972 Olympic skiing gold medallist Bernard Russi. He told me a simple rule that he found enabled him to elevate himself above the other great racers of his time: One more thing, one more time. He assumed that all of his competitors were working hard physically, technically, and mentally. So, every time he came to the end of a workout, he said to himself, "One more thing, one more time." He would then do one more sprint or one more set of weights or take one more training run. By doing one more thing, one more time, he believed he was doing that little bit more than his competitors that would separate himself from them on race day.

The value of mistakes. Perhaps the most frustrating part of sports is all the mistakes you make as you develop as an athlete. Most athletes view mistakes as failure. Athletes often see mistakes as a personal attack on their ability as an athlete and their worth as a person. As I described in Chapter Six, for many athletes, making mistakes is unacceptable and a source of frustration and other negative emotions.

Most athletes don't realize that the best athletes in the world make mistakes all of the time. What makes these athletes great is not that they don't make mistakes, but rather it is the attitude they have about their mistakes and how they respond to those they do make. Mistakes only mean failure if athletes don't learn from them and if they keep repeating them.

Mistakes are a natural and necessary part of becoming a better athlete. They really mean that you're becoming more successful because you're moving out of your comfort zone. Mistakes mean you're working to improve. They are also valuable information showing you what you need to work on. If you're not making mistakes, you're not pushing yourself to become a better athlete. They indicate that you're taking risks, going for it, and doing something new. Mistakes mean success when you learn from them and you stop repeating them.

What is ironic is that most athletes' attitudes toward mistakes actually increase the likelihood that they will continue. By getting frustrated and discouraged, athletes are more likely to make more mistakes because they become tentative, doubtful, anxious, and focused on failure. Learning from your mistakes, and not repeating them, involves knowing how to respond to the mistakes you make. You need to learn to respond in a positive and constructive way.

The goal is to reduce the number of mistakes you make in practice by figuring out how to correct them and ingraining the proper execution. The first step is to identify what you're doing wrong that is causing the mistake. For example, if a soccer player is consistently kicking the ball over the goal post. Next, you can specify what you need to do to correct the problem. In the case of the soccer player, she needs to keep her head down and her weight more forward. Then, when you prepare to execute the skill again, you can focus on the correction, which should solve the problem that's leading to the mistake being repeated.

Get out of your comfort zone. Most athletes like to stay in their comfort zone. They like to perform the way they usually do and they get uncomfortable if they try to do anything differently. This approach might make them feel good, but the problem is that they'll never perform their best or move up to a new level.

To become your best, you must move out of your comfort zone. This means making changes to your performances that will help you in the future. For example, a hockey goalie's comfort zone is staying in the crease. If he want to get better, he needs to develop the ability to come out of the crease, when necessary, to cut off the angle or challenge a breakaway. The risk of moving out of your comfort zone is that you'll make some mistakes at first and might perform poorly and lose for a while. But as you do it more, you become more skilled and familiar with it, until you reach a point at which it's no longer uncomfortable. Before you know it, you've raised your comfort zone and your performances to a new level.

Never give up. There's a tendency among many athletes to give up in practice when they're not performing well. They might shorten their drilling because they just can't get the new technique or they stop trying because they're not performing well. Athletes rationalize giving up by saying that training doesn't really count for anything. My twelve laws of preparation would argue otherwise. Training matters because everything athletes practice either contributes to or interferes with developing effective competitive skills and habits.

If athletes give up in training, they're learning the skill of giving up. If they practice giving up in training, when they perform poorly in a competition, their learned skill will be to give up. The skill of never giving up is so important because something rather important happens every time athletes give up: They automatically lose. If athletes keep fighting, they may not win, but at least they have a chance. Athletes want to ingrain the skill of performing at 100% and never giving up no matter what happens during a competition.

> *"Only concentrated practice helps toward excellence. Practice without focus or without knowledge of what you're doing is worthless."*
>
> **Professional bowler Andy Varipapa**

CHAPTER EIGHT

PRIME SPORT ROUTINES

Routines are one of the most important aspects of sports that athletes can develop to improve their training and competitive performances. The fundamental value of routines is that they ensure total preparation in athletes' efforts. Routines enable athletes to be completely physically, technically, tactically, and mentally ready to perform their best. I don't know a world-class athlete in any sport who does not use routines in some part of his or her competitive preparations.

Routines are most often used before competitions to make sure that athletes are prepared to perform their best. They can also be valuable in two other areas. Routines can be developed in training to ensure that athletes get the most out of their practice time. Routines are also important between performances of a competition to help athletes get ready for subsequent performances (for sports comprised of a series of short performances).

There are a lot of things in sport that athletes can't control such as weather conditions and their opponent. Ultimately, the only thing athletes can control is themselves. Sport routines can increase control over their performances by enabling them to directly prepare every area that impacts their sport. Those areas athletes can control include their equipment (is your gear in optimal condition?), their body (are you physically and technically warmed up?), and their mind (are you at prime focus and intensity?).

Routines also allow athletes to make their preparation more predictable by knowing they're systematically covering every area that will influence performance. Athletes can also expect the unexpected. In other words, they can plan for every eventuality that could arise during a competition. If athletes can reduce the things that can go wrong and be prepared for those things that do, they'll be better able to stayed focused and relaxed before and during the competition.

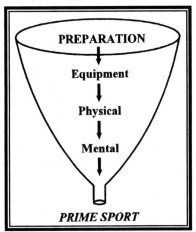

All of your preparation involves a consistent narrowing of effort, energy, and focus. Each step closer to performing should lead you to that unique state of readiness in which you are physically and mentally ready to perform your best. You can think of your preparation as a funnel. Whatever you put into the funnel will dictate what comes out. If you put good preparation into the funnel, what will come out is good sports performance. I call this the Prime Sport Funnel.

Some sport psychologists use the term, ritual, in place of routine. I don't like this term because it has connotations that go against what routines are trying to accomplish. Remember, the goal of routines is to totally prepare athletes for training or competition. Everything done in a routine serves a specific and practical function in that readiness process. For example, a physical and technical warm-up and a review of tactics for an upcoming competition are all essential for total preparation.

In contrast, a ritual is associated with superstitions and is often made up of things that have no practical impact on performance, for instance, wearing lucky socks or following a specific route to the competition site. Routines can also be adjusted should the need arise, for example, if you arrive late to the competition, you can shorten your routine and still get prepared. Rituals, though, are rigid and ceremonial. Athletes can believe that rituals must be done or they will not perform well. You control routines, but rituals control you.

"I attach a great deal to mental preparation before a final."

Chris Evert

BENEFITS OF SPORT ROUTINES

Sport routines have many benefits to training and competition. Foremost, they develop consistency in all areas that impact your sport. By consistently going through your sport routine, you're training your mind and body to respond the same way regardless of the situation. As my seventh law of preparation suggests, consistent preparation leads to consistent thinking, intensity, focus, emotions, and physical and technical readiness, which will result in Prime Sport.

At the same time, consistency does not mean rigidity. Routines are flexible. They can be adjusted to different situations that arise, for example, a delay in the start of your competition. Flexibility in your routine means you won't be surprised or stressed by changes that occur during your preparations. Flexibility means you'll be better able to perform your best in a wider range of performing situations and conditions. Ultimately, the goal of routines in training and competition is to ensure that when you begin, you're totally physically, technically, tactically, and mentally prepared to perform your best.

"To repeat successes of the past, you follow your old program. Don't get fancy; just be consistent."

Former Olympic marathoner Bill Rodgers

TRAINING ROUTINES

Developing sport routines should begin in practice. For you to get the most out of your training, you should develop a brief training routine that will ensure that you're totally prepared for every drill. The first step in your training routine is getting your body ready. This involves checking and adjusting your intensity as needed. This might mean taking deep breaths to calm yourself down or using intense breaths to raise your intensity. I recommend that before every drill you move your feet and bounce up and down to get your body going in preparation for the start of the drill. Second, you need to focus on what you want to work on in the drill. If you have an internal focus style, your Mag-Lite® beam should already be narrow and focused on a particular cue. If you have an external focus style, this would be the time to narrow your beam onto the cue. To narrow your focus, you can remind yourself what is the purpose of the drill. Then, you can repeat your keyword. At this point as the drill begins, your body and your mind are ready to perform Prime Sport.

Your training routine need only last a few seconds, but will completely prepare you to get the most out of your training. It will also lay the foundation for using sport routines before and during competitions. Remember, for your training routine to become effective, you must use it every time you begin a drill.

"I only play well when I'm prepared. If I don't practice the way I should, then I won't play the way that I know I can."

Tennis great Ivan Lendl

PRE-COMPETITIVE ROUTINES

The next step in developing effective sport routines is to create a pre-competitive routine that is an extended version of the training routine. The goal is the same, to be totally prepared to perform your best. The difference is that a pre-competitive routine will dictate how you perform in your upcoming competition and it can take up to several hours to complete.

There is no one ideal routine for everyone. Pre-competitive routines are individual. For every great athlete, you'll see a different routine, but all will have common elements. You have to decide what exactly to put into your routine and how to structure it. Developing an effective pre-competitive routine is a progressive process that will take time before you have one that really works for you.

Focus and intensity are two areas that you must consider in developing your pre-competitive routine. You already know whether you have an internal or external focus style and you know what level of intensity at which you perform best. With that in mind, you want to plan your pre-competitive routine so that when you begin a competition, you have prime focus and intensity.

Focus needs. The goal in your pre-competitive routine if you have an internal focus style is to put yourself in a place where there are few external distractions and where you can focus on your pre-competitive preparation. To maintain that narrow Mag-Lite® beam, you want to go through your pre-competitive routine away from other people and activities that could distract you.

An external focus style means that you need to keep your Mag-Lite® beam wide during your preparations so you can keep your mind off the upcoming competition and away from thinking too much. The goal in your pre-competitive routine if you have an external focus style is to put yourself in a place where you're unable to become focused internally and think about the competition. Your pre-competitive routine should be done where there is enough activity to draw your focus away from inside your head. To widen the beam, you want to go through your pre-competitive routine around people and activities that can draw your focus outward.

Intensity needs. You'll also want to build your pre-competitive routine around your intensity needs. The intensity component of your pre-competitive routine should include checking your intensity periodically before the approaching competition and using psych-up or psych-down techniques to adjust it as needed. You'll need to set aside time in your routine when you can do these techniques. As you approach the competition, you'll want to move closer to your prime intensity. The short period just before the competition should be devoted to a final check and adjustment of your intensity.

If you perform best at a lower level of intensity, you want your pre-competitive routine to be done at an easy pace and have plenty of opportunities to take a break to slow down and relax. You'll want to be around people who are relaxed and low-key as well. If you're around anxious people, they'll make you nervous too.

If you perform best at a higher level of intensity, you want your pre-competitive routine to be done at a faster pace with more energy put into the components of your routine. You will want to make sure that you are constantly doing something. There should be little time during which you are just standing around and waiting. You'll also want to be around people who are energetic and outgoing.

Music. Music is a powerful tool you can use to assist in your pre-competitive preparations. It can help you achieve both prime focus and prime intensity. Music can also positively impact your emotions. Listening to music can help you adjust your Mag-Lite® beam. You can use music as a way of narrowing your Mag-Lite® beam by drawing your focus away from what is happening around you. If you're focused on your music, you won't be paying attention to your surroundings. Music is also a way for you to widen your Mag-Lite® beam by drawing your focus outside of your head. If you're listening to music, you're less likely to be thinking too much about your competition.

As I discussed in Chapter Four, music can have a similar impact on your intensity. We all know how powerful music can be. Music has the ability to soothe us or get us fired up. In this way, you can use music to help adjust your intensity. If you need to lower your intensity, you should listen to calming music. If you need to raise your intensity, you should listen to high-energy music.

You can also use music to alter your emotions. Music has the power to inspire us, to excite us, or to make us sad or angry. By listening to the right kind of music, you can actively create the emotions you want to perform your best. For example, hard rock will energize and motivate you or classical music will make you feel happy and content.

Designing a pre-competitive routine. The first step in designing a pre-competitive routine is to make a list of everything you need to do before a competition to be prepared. Some of the common elements you should include are meals, review of competitive tactics, physical warm-up, technical warm-up, equipment check, and mental preparation. Other more personal things that might go into a pre-competitive routine include going to the bathroom, changing into your competition clothing, and using mental imagery.

Then, decide in what order you want to do the components of your list as you approach the start of the competition. In doing this, consider competition activities that might need to be taken into account. For instance, availability of a warm-up area or a place where you can eat your pre-competitive meal can influence when you accomplish different parts of your pre-competitive routine.

Next, specify where each step of your routine can best be completed. You should use your knowledge of competitive sites at which you often perform to figure this part out. For example, if you like to be alone before a competition, is there a quiet place you can get away from people?

Finally, establish a time frame and a schedule for completing your routine. In other words, how much time do you need to get totally prepared? Some athletes like to get to the competition site only a short time before they begin. Others like to arrive hours before. All of these decisions are personal. You need to find out what works best for you. Use the Personalized Sport Routine form (see page 122) to assist you in developing your pre-competitive routine.

Once your pre-competitive routine is organized, try it out at competitions. Some things may work and others may not. In time, you'll be able to fine-tune your routine until you find the one that's most comfortable and best prepares you for competition. Lastly, remember, pre-competitive routines only have value if they're used consistently. If you use your routine before every competition, in a short time, you won't even have to think about doing it. Your pre-competitive routine will simply be what you do before each competition and it will ensure that you are totally prepared to perform your best.

"There isn't a pro who doesn't recognize the value of a routine and who doesn't use one."

Professional golfer Curtis Strange

PERSONALIZED PRE-COMPETITIVE ROUTINE

Directions: List the pre-competitive activities that will help you to totally prepare to perform your best.

Early in Day

    1.   Physical:

    2.   Mental:

At Competitive Site

    1.   Physical:

    2.   Mental:

Final Preparation

    1.   Equipment:

    2.   Physical:

    3.   Mental:

COMPETITIVE ROUTINES

Many sports, including baseball, football, tennis golf, track and field, and many others, are comprised of a series of short performances. For these sports, being well-prepared for the first performance is not enough. Competitive routines can be invaluable in ensuring that athletes are prepared for every performance in a competition. One thing that I found that separates the great athletes from the good ones is their ability to be consistently ready for every performance. By being totally prepared for every performance, you can be sure that you won't give your opponent "free points" because you weren't ready.

The time between performances is essential to consistent competitive performance. What you think, feel, and do between performances often dictates how you perform. You must take control of the time between performances to be sure that you're totally prepared.

I use a four-step competitive routine called the Four R's. The first R is *rest*. Immediately after the conclusion of the previous performance, take several slow, deep breaths and let your muscles relax. This is especially important after a long or demanding performance in which you become fatigued and out of breath. It's also important near the end of a long competition in which you're tired and need to recover as much as possible to be ready for the next performance. Deep breathing and relaxing also help you center yourself and better prepare you for the next R.

The second R is *regroup*. This phase of the competitive routine addresses your emotions between performances. Particularly when you are not performing well or the competition is at a critical juncture, you may feel a variety of emotions such as excitement, frustration, anger, or depression. Regrouping allows you to gain awareness of how your emotions are impacting you and, if they are affecting you negatively, to master them so they help rather than hurt you in the next performance. If you are emotional after a poor performance, you may feel frustrated and angry. You should give yourself more time to regroup and let go of the unhealthy emotions. Because of the powerful influence emotions have on your performances, your ability to "get your act together" emotionally between performances may be the most important thing you can do to prepare for the next performance.

An important realization that can make regrouping easier is that performances in a competition are not directly related to each other. In other words, the chances of being successful in the next performance are in no way associated with how you performed in the last performance. For example, a poor parallel bars routine by a gymnast has no direct bearing on how he performs on the pommel horse.

One thing that connects performances are the emotions attached to the last performance. If you're frustrated and angry about your last performance, you increase your chances of doing poorly in the next performance because negative emotions usually interfere with good performances. In contrast, if you have positive emotions about the last performance, you increase your chances of succeeding in the next performance because positive emotions will make you more motivated and confident which, in turn, will enable you to perform better. Using the time to regroup will enable you to let go of and replace the negative emotions with positive ones, thereby increasing your chances of having a successful performance.

The third R is *refocus*. There can be a tendency during competitions, especially in pressure situations, to focus on the last performance or the outcome of the competition, none of which will help you perform well. This is a form of outcome focus in which you're focusing on the unsuccessful outcome of the last performance or the possible result at the end of the competition. When this happens, you need to return to a process focus for the next performance. During the refocus phase of the competitive routine, you should first evaluate your present situation, for example, the score, how you've been performing, and tactics. Then, focus on what you need to for the next performance. Your focus may be technical, tactical, or mental. The important thing is to begin the next performance with a clear focus on what you want to do to perform your best.

The fourth R is *recharge*. If your body is not prepared, you won't be able to perform your best. Just prior to beginning the performance, you should check and adjust your intensity. If you need to lower your intensity, you should slow your pace, take deep breaths, and relax your muscles. If you need to raise your intensity, you should increase your pace, take some short, intense breaths, and jump up and down.

> *"You have to do the same thing every time you go to the line, whether it's dribble three times, take a deep breath, or whatever."*
>
> **NBA player Dennis Scott**

CHAPTER NINE

PRIME SPORT IMAGERY

Sport imagery is one of the most powerful tools athletes can use to improve their sports performances. It's used by virtually all great athletes and there is considerable scientific research supporting its value. This research indicates that using sport imagery alone produces gains in performance. More importantly, combining actual practice with sport imagery results in more improvement than practice alone.

Sport imagery is so beneficial because it impacts every contributor to Prime Sport. It improves every part of the Prime Sport pyramid. Sport imagery increases motivation by allowing athletes to see and feel themselves working hard and reaching their goals. It builds confidence by enabling athletes to see and feel themselves performing well and succeeding. Sport imagery improves intensity by allowing athletes to imagine experiencing pressure and using psych-up or psych-down techniques to control it. It enhances focus by identifying important cues and letting athletes rehearse prime focus. Finally, sport imagery enables athletes to generate positive emotions in response to seeing and feeling themselves perform their best.

Sport imagery also improves technical, tactical, and competitive development. It ingrains the image and feeling of correct technique and provides imagined repetition of proper execution. Sport imagery also enables athletes to further learn sound tactics and instill effective competitive skills, habits, and routines. Finally, it ingrains the image and feeling of athletes performing their best.

126

Sport imagery can be used in several settings that will help athletes achieve Prime Sport. During practice, athletes can use it to facilitate their technical development and improve the quality of their training. Away from their sport, athletes can use sport imagery to complement their practice efforts and as part of their pre-competitive routine.

> *"Of all our faculties the most important one is our ability to imagine."*
>
> ### Wilt Chamberlain

SPORT IMAGERY IS A SKILL

It's important to understand that sport imagery is a skill, just like a technical skill, that develops with practice. Few athletes have perfect sport imagery when they first use it. It's common for athletes who haven't used sport imagery before to struggle with it at first. This discourages them and leads them to believe that sport imagery can't be beneficial. If athletes put in the time and effort, their sport imagery will improve and it will become a valuable tool for them.

The first thing you want to do is assess your imagery abilities. To do this, complete the Sport Imagery Profile (see page 129). It will give a graphic representation of your sport imagery strengths and areas in need of improvement. Using this information, you can emphasize and strengthen the areas in need of work in your sport imagery program. The next section will describe each factor in more detail and provide exercises to improve each imagery area.

> *"I'd try to create an instant replay on the inside of my eyelids. Usually I'd catch only part of the particular move the first time I tried this. But the next time I saw the move I'd catch a little more of it, so that soon I could call up a complete picture."*
>
> ### Bill Russell

SPORT IMAGERY FACTORS

Perspective—Internal imagery (from inside your body looking out) or external imagery (from outside your body like watching yourself on video) or both. (1-all internal; 5-both; 10-all external)

Control—Control of your images as you perform (e.g., perform well with an accurate image of how you perform or difficulty imagining how you perform or making mistakes in your imagery). (1-no control; 10-total control)

Visual—How clearly you see yourself performing (e.g., see all aspects of performance). (1-unclear; 10-clear)

Auditory—How clearly you hear sounds associated with your sport (e.g., ball hitting bat, shoes against court, skates on ice). (1-unclear; 10-clear)

Physical feeling—How clearly you feel yourself performing (e.g., muscles working, court under your feet, water against your skin). (1-unclear; 10-clear)

Thoughts—How well you are able to reproduce the thoughts that you have when you are performing (e.g., about technique, tactics, positive or negative). (1-no thoughts; 10-usual thoughts)

Emotions—How well you are able to reproduce the emotions that you feel when you are performing (e.g., excitement, frustration, anger, depression). (1-no emotions; 10-strong emotions)

Total image—How well you are able to accurately reproduce the competitive experience (e.g., all of the senses, thoughts, emotions, and physical feelings). (1-poor reproduction; 10-exact reproduction)

Speed—Your ability to speed up or slow down your imagery. (1-not all; 10-easily)

SPORT IMAGERY PROFILE

Name _____   Date _____

Directions: Nine factors that are important for sport imagery are identified in the profile below. Before rating yourself on each factor, close your eyes and imagine performing for 30 seconds, paying attention to a particular factor. Indicate how you perceive yourself on the 1-10 scale for each factor by drawing a line at that rating number and shading in the area toward the center of the profile. Except for Perspective , a score below a <u>7</u> indicates an area in need of improvement.

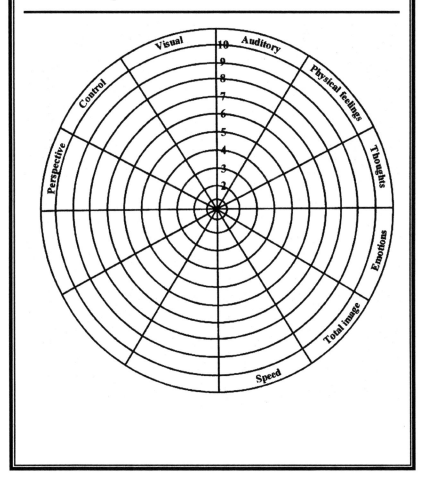

MAXIMIZING SPORT IMAGERY

There are seven factors that will impact the quality of your sport imagery: perspective, control, multiple sense, thoughts, emotions, total image, and speed. Each of these areas can be developed with practice.

Imagery perspective. Imagery perspective refers to where the "imagery camera" is when you do sport imagery. You will use one of two perspectives. The internal perspective involves seeing yourself from inside your body looking out, as if you were actually performing. The imagery camera is inside your head looking out through your eyes. The external perspective involves seeing yourself from outside your body like on video. The imagery camera follows your performance from the outside.

Research indicates that one perspective is not better than the other. Rather, most people have a dominant perspective with which they're most comfortable. There are also some people who are equally adept at both perspectives. You should use the perspective that's most natural for you and then experiment with the other perspective to see if it helps you in a different way.

Try this exercise. Imagine yourself performing your sport four times for 30 seconds. The first two times use your dominant perspective. The next two times use the other perspective. You may find that only one perspective works for you or you may find that you can use either perspective equally well. In either case, for the time being, rely on the perspective that comes most naturally to you.

Control. Have you ever been doing sport imagery and you keep making mistakes? This problem relates to imagery control, which is how well you're able to imagine what you want to imagine. It's not uncommon for athletes new to sport imagery to perform poorly in their imagery. This can be frustrating because if you can't imagine good performances in your head, you're probably going to have a difficult time performing well in real life.

Imagery control is a skill that develops with practice. If mistakes occur in your imagery, you shouldn't just let them go by. If you do, you'll ingrain the negative image and feeling which will hurt your performances. Instead, when you perform poorly in your imagery, immediately rewind the "imagery video" and edit it. That is, rerun the imagery video until you do it correctly.

Try this exercise. Imagine yourself performing five times for 30 seconds. In each segment, if you make a mistake, rewind and edit your imagery until you get it right. I've sometimes found it difficult for athletes to edit their imagery when they imagine themselves performing at full speed. It can be helpful when they're having difficulty controlling their imagery to slow their imagery down, in which they see and feel themselves performing in slow motion. This technique seems to enable athletes to have greater control of their imagery. As they gain better control of their imagery in slow motion, they can progressively increase the speed of their imagery while maintaining good control until they're able to perform well at "real time" speed.

Multiple senses. You may have noticed that I use the word imagery rather than visualization to describe this technique. This is because visualization places too much emphasis on its visual component. Good sport imagery is more than just visual. The best imagery involves the multi-sensory reproduction of the actual sports experience. You should see, hear, and feel your sport imagery.

Visual imagery involves how clearly you see yourself performing. Ideally, your visual images should be as clear as if you are actually performing. It may be, though, that your images are blurry or you can't see yourself at all.

In order to imagine yourself performing, you must know what you look like performing in your sport. If you can't produce an accurate image of how you perform, you will probably imagine yourself performing like someone you train with or like a top athlete in your sport. In either case, the images will not help you because they will be inconsistent with how you actually perform.

Try this exercise. Watch yourself performing on video, then immediately close your eyes and reproduce the video images. As the visual image of how you perform becomes more clear, put away the video for a while and repeat the accurate visual images of your performances. If the image starts to fade, return to the video until you're able to see yourself performing consistently. This exercise will help you ingrain an accurate image of how you perform.

Vivid auditory images are important because sounds can play an important part in sports performance. For example, a swimmer hears a competitor catching up to her in the next lane or labored breathing by opponents lets you know that they are getting tired. Negative talk from opponents tells you that they're becoming discouraged.

Try this exercise. Imagine performing three times for 30 seconds. Each time, focus on a different sound associated with performance in your sport. Once you're able to do this consistently, put all of the sounds together and hear the various sounds in one sequence of sport imagery.

I believe that the most powerful part of sport imagery is feeling it in your body. That's how you really ingrain new technical and mental skills and habits. A useful way to increase the feeling in your sport imagery is to combine imagined and real sensations. Imagine yourself performing and move your body with the imagined performance. By integrating the imagined sensations with the actual physical feelings, you can improve the value of sport imagery even more.

Try this exercise. Imagine performing two times for 30 seconds. Each time, focus on feeling your muscles and the physical movements. Then, imagine performing two more times focusing on the feeling, but this time, move your body with the imagery to simulate the actual movement, for example, a basketball player shooting a jump shot. By combining the imagined feelings with the actual physical feelings, you'll further enhance the quality of your sport imagery and increase its benefits.

Thoughts. What you think during a competition often dictates your intensity, emotions, and how you perform. Sport imagery gives you the ability to learn new and better ways of thinking during competitions. You can generate competitive situations in your imagery in which you have displayed negative self-talk and body language. Drawing on the techniques described in Chapter Three, you can replace the negative self-talk and body language with positive expressions that will help you achieve Prime Sport. Using sport imagery in this way enables you to gain the added repetition of positive thinking that will further ingrain new positive thinking skills.

Try this exercise. Imagine yourself in a competitive situation in which you have negative self-talk and body language. Allow yourself to experience the negative thoughts and body language, then imagine yourself replacing the negatives with positive expressions using thought-stopping, positive keywords, and positive body language. Then, imagine yourself performing well.

Emotions. Emotions play an important role in your ability to achieve Prime Sport. Incorporating them into sport imagery can be a valuable way to ingrain positive emotions into your competitive performances. Much like in actual competitions, imagining scenarios that have in the past evoked negative emotions gives you the opportunity to respond to them in an emotionally different way.

Try this exercise. Imagine yourself in a competitive situation in which you feel negative emotions, for example, you get frustrated when you make a mistake. Allow yourself to experience the frustration and then project yourself ahead and replace the negative emotions with positive ones that will help you perform better.

Total image. Another key aspect of sport imagery is being able to imagine the total performance. The most effective imagery reproduces every aspect of the actual sports performance. In your sport imagery, you should duplicate the sights, sounds, physical sensations, thoughts, and emotions that you would experience at an actual competition.

Try this exercise. Imagine yourself performing five times for 30 seconds. In each segment, choose a different aspect of the performance to focus on, for example, visual, auditory, physical feeling, thoughts, and emotions. Emphasize experiencing that part of the sports experience. Then, imagine performing five more times. In these performances, combine all the aspects of sport imagery and imagine the total performance. The more you can exactly reproduce the actual sports experience, the more you'll get from your sport imagery.

Speed. The ability to adjust the speed of your imagery will enable you to use sport imagery to improve different aspects of your performance. Slow motion is effective for focusing on technique. During actual training, it's difficult to work on technique at full speed. Instead, you begin technical change at slow speed under easy conditions. The same thing works for sport imagery. When you first start to work on technique in your imagery, slow the imagery video down, frame by frame if necessary, to see yourself executing the skill correctly. Then slowly increase the speed of your imagery to "real time" until you're able to execute the technique at full speed.

You can use high-speed sport imagery to improve your speed and reactions. Just as in actual training, thoughts and external distractions can interfere with performance. It can be difficult to maintain focus and rely on your reactions to perform well. Similarly, in imagery, thoughts can intrude and can hurt focus and the imagined performance. Use fast motion imagery to develop better focus and to improve your reactions. Speed up your sport imagery so you don't have time to be distracted. High-speed imagery reduces thinking, primes reactions, and hones automatic performance.

Try this exercise. Choose a technique you're working on in your sport. Imagine performing the technique six times. The first two times, slow down the imagery so you can really focus on doing it correctly. If you can do the technique properly at slow speed, increase the speed to a moderate rate. If you can do the technique correctly at a moderate speed, increase the imagery to full speed. You know you have the technique ingrained in your mind and body when you can do it correctly at high speed.

> *"When I am running hard, I visualize myself running my goal race. I also visualize myself from an outsider's view. I visualize myself finishing the race with that elated feeling and running a really great time."*
>
> **Runner Jerry Lawson**

SPORT IMAGERY FOR PRIME TRAINING

There are several places you can incorporate sport imagery into your training. Just before you begin a drill, instead of thinking about what you want to work on, see and feel yourself doing it with sport imagery. Close your eyes and briefly imagine how you want to perform the drill. This will increase your focus on the purpose of the drill and give you a positive image and feeling that will help its execution.

You can also use sport imagery when you've finished a drill. If you just had a great drill in which you performed well, the most important thing you want to do is remember the image and feeling. So right after the drill, close your eyes and replay the drill with sport imagery. This will ingrain the positive image and feeling.

If you just had a poor drill in which you made mistakes, the dominant feeling and image is negative. The last thing you want to do is remember it. Yet, that is the image and feeling in your mind and body, and it is what will come out when you begin your next drill. You need to flush out the negative image and feeling. Right after the drill, edit your sport imagery, this time performing the drill well. This editing process clears out the negative image and feeling and replaces it with positive ones.

You can also use sport imagery after your coach has given you instruction. Typically, a coach will give you feedback and then will tell you to think about it before you begin the next drill. But where does thinking occur? In your head. Where does performing occur? In your body. Thinking about instruction doesn't always translate into the body effectively. Sport imagery acts as a bridge between the thoughts in your mind and the actions in your body. You can use sport imagery to ingrain the instruction into your mind and body. After your coach gives you instruction, close your eyes and imagine yourself making the correction that you were just told.

> *"I'm visualizing every single part of the downhill course. I want it to be totally rehearsed in my head."*
>
> **Olympic ski racer Chad Fleischer**

SPORT IMAGERY FOR COMPETITION

Sport imagery can be a valuable tool during competitions. If you're performing poorly and need to make a correction, instead of thinking about what you need to do to correct it, use sport imagery. Between performances, close your eyes and imagine yourself performing the way you want. Be sure to focus on the correction in your imagery and to see and feel yourself doing it properly. Using sport imagery in this way will give you confidence that you can perform successfully again, generate positive emotions that will make you feel better, and increase your focus on the change. It will also take your mind off of negative thoughts and feelings that may have arisen in response to the poor performance.

Sport imagery can also be used to change strategy during a competition. Rather than thinking about a change in tactics, for example, deciding to be more aggressive, imagine yourself performing that way. This approach allows you to practice your change in strategy before you actually use it.

> *"Before a jump, I'll rock back and forth, close my eyes and envision the perfect jump."*
>
> **World-class pentathlete Gwen Wentland**

DEVELOPING A SPORT IMAGERY PROGRAM

A sport imagery program allows athletes to systematically address key areas they need to improve in their sport. Athletes can use sport imagery to consistently develop technical, tactical, and mental aspects of their sports performance.

Sport imagery goals. The first step in developing a sport imagery program is to set goals. They could be technical, such as improving execution of a skill in your sport, tactical, such as being more patient early in a competition, mental, such as increasing your confidence or reducing your intensity, or relate to overall performance, such as improving your consistency. Use the Sport Imagery Goals form (see page 138) to identify the areas on which you want to work.

SPORT IMAGERY GOALS

Name _____   **Date** _____

Directions: In the space below, indicate your goals for your sport imagery program. Be specific in identifying ar eas where you want to improve your sport.

Technical

       1.

       2.

Tactical

       1.

       2.

Mental

       1.

       2.

Overall Performance

       1.

       2.

Sport imagery ladder. The next step involves creating a sport imagery performance ladder. You wouldn't begin to change a part of your performance in an important competition. Rather, you would start off practicing new skills in a practice situation where mistakes don't matter. Similarly, you don't want to begin your sport imagery program in a big imagined competition. Using the Sport Imagery Ladder form (see page 140), create a ladder of practice and competitive situations in which you'll be performing. The ladder should start with the least important practice situation and increase up to the most important competition in which you will perform. For example, a low rung of the Sport Imagery Ladder could be performing your sport with a friend and the highest rung could be performing in a championship. This ladder enables you to work on areas you've identified in increasingly more demanding situations.

You should begin your sport imagery program at the lowest rung of the ladder and work your way up until you've reached the highest rung. Don't move up to the next rung until you can perform the way you want at the current rung. Once you feel good at a particular rung, stay there for several imagery sessions to reinforce the positive images, thoughts, and feelings.

SPORT IMAGERY LADDER

Name _____   **Date** _____

Directions: In the space below, create a ladder of practice and competitive situations in which you will imagine yourself. The ladder should increase incrementally in terms of importance. Specify the performing situation (e.g., drilling, practice, or competition). Examples are italicized.

Least Important

     1. *(performing with a friend)*

     2. *(drilling with coach)*

Moderately Important

     3. *(practice competition)*

     4. *(low-level competition)*

Most Important

     5. *(major competition)*

Create sport imagery scenarios. Once you've established your goals and built your sport imagery ladder, you're ready to create practice and competitive scenarios that you will follow in your sport imagery sessions (see Sport Imagery Scenarios on page 142). These scenarios are actual practice or competitive situations in which you can work on your technical, tactical, mental, and performance goals.

If you perform in a sport such as figure skating and gymnastics in which competitive performances last, at most, a few minutes, you can not imagine yourself performing an entire performance. If you perform in a sport, like hockey or baseball, that lasts a long time, it would be unrealistic for you to imagine an entire performance. Instead, you should identify four or five performance situations that are realistic. For example, a football running back might imagine running a variety of plays in practice in which he is the ball carrier. As he moves up the sport imagery ladder, he could imagine running those plays in increasingly more important games.

It's important that your imagery scenarios are practice or competition specific. You shouldn't just imagine yourself performing in a nonspecific location, event, and under undefined conditions. Rather, you should imagine a practice or competition scenario in which you perform at a particular site, in a specific event, against a identifiable opponent. Also, be sure that the events, locations, conditions, and opponents are appropriate for your level of performance. For example, if you're a junior athlete, you shouldn't imagine yourself competing against Roger Clemens, Brandi Chastain, Alonzo Mourning, or Martina Hingis.

SPORT IMAGERY SCENARIOS

Name _____   **Date** _____

Directions: In the space below, create several practice and competitive scenarios that you can follow in your sport imagery sessions as you climb your sport imagery ladder. These scenarios should provide you with detailed descriptions of what you want to imagine as you work on some part of your sport in training and competition.

Training

Competition

Sport imagery log. Since sport imagery is not tangible like, for example, weight lifting where you can see how much weight you've lifted or sprints where you can be timed, it's useful to keep a log of your sport imagery sessions. By recording your sport imagery sessions, you'll be able to see improvement as you make your way up the ladder. Use the Sport Imagery Log (see page 144) to record relevant aspects of your imagery sessions.

The first piece of information you should record is the *rung* of the sport imagery ladder. Place a number between one and five to indicate where you are in your climb up the ladder. Rate the *quality* of the imagery session on a 1-10 scale. How clear were the images, how well did you perform, how did you feel about the imagery session?

Describe your *performance*, that is, what you worked on and what you actually imagined during the imagery session. Specify the *number of mistakes* you made in the imagery session. Then indicate what *type of mistakes* you made most frequently.

Rate the quality of your *senses* in your imagery session. Assign yourself a 1-10 score for how clear was the visual, auditory, and physical imagery you experienced. Lastly, evaluate the *mental* aspects of your imagery by briefly describing relevant thoughts and emotions you had during your imagery session. The emphasis of this area should be on how positive or negative were your thoughts and emotions.

Practical concerns. You should structure your sport imagery sessions into your daily routine. If you schedule them for the same time every day, you're more likely to remember to do them. Find a quiet, comfortable place where you won't be disturbed. Each session should last no longer than 10 minutes. Do sport imagery three to four times a week. Like any form of training, if you do it too much, you'll get tired of it. Finally, start your sport imagery sessions with one of the relaxation procedures that I described in Chapter Four. The deep state of relaxation will help you generate better quality images and it will make you more receptive to the images and feelings you're trying to ingrain.

SPORT IMAGERY LOG

DATE	LADDER: #of rung	QUALITY: 1-10	PERFORMANCE: What you imagined	CONTROL: # & type of mistakes	SENSES: Visual—Auditory— Physical	MENTAL: Thoughts and emotions

Chapter Ten

Prime Competition

The result of achieving Prime Sport is what I call a Prime Competition, when you're able to perform your best from the start of a competition to its conclusion. This is one of the characteristics that differentiates the best athletes in the world, and the athletes at any level who win consistently, from those who are less successful. Prime Competition athletes are able to maintain a high level of performance throughout a competition with few letdowns. I found three distinct stages that determined whether an athlete could accomplish a Prime Competition.

Prime start. The first stage I call Prime Start. One of the first lessons that emerged from my work with world-class and professional athletes was that they could not afford to start slowly. It is not uncommon for athletes from weekend warriors to juniors to the world's best to believe that they can settle into the competition during its early stages, then really turn it on. In a sense, this approach is making a fundamental mistake: athletes are using the beginning of the competition as a warm-up. Against a tough opponent in an important competition, this will not work. The competition is simply not the time to get warmed up.

If you're performing against someone whom you are better than, then you can fall behind and once you get going, you'll be able to catch up and defeat them. However, these competitions are not why you're striving to achieve Prime Sport. The real meaning of experiencing Prime Sport is that you're competing against an opponent who is as good or better than you in a competition that matters to you. Against this athlete a slow start will be a kiss of death. You will not be able to work your way into the competition. If you try this, you will find that you will be behind before you know it and your opponent is too good and too tough to let you back into the competition.

Having a prime start goes back to many themes I have discussed throughout this book, most notably, being totally prepared to perform your best from the very start of the competition. Your ability to experience a prime start depends on whether you're physically, technically, tactically, and mentally ready to achieve Prime Sport from the start of the competition.

At the heart of this readiness is your pre-competitive routine. It should ensure that you are completely ready to perform at your highest level from the onset of the competition. There are several key components to making sure this happens. First, you must have a good physical warm-up. If your body is not prepared, you will not be able to have a prime start to the competition. Your physical warm-up should include everything necessary to ensure total physical readiness. Common physical warm-up activities in many sports include a short run, jumping rope, stretching, and agility and footwork drills. This part of the pre-competitive routine will also help you move toward your prime intensity.

For technical sports such as tennis, golf, and figure skating, the next step in your pre-competitive preparations should be your technical warm-up. This is a process by which you execute every skill that you will use in the competition repeatedly until you are confident and comfortable. This is an area where I see many athletes fall short. Most technical warm-ups I see are unstructured and unfocused, in which athletes half-heartedly and incompletely run through their technical repertoire and deem themselves warmed up.

A technical warm-up that leads to a prime start should be organized and comprehensive, systematically covering every skill that is necessary to achieve Prime Sport. The last few executions of a skill should be performed with competitive focus and intensity. This last step enables you to performance the first technique of the competition with absolute confidence, comfort, and quality.

The final step of the prime start warm-up is to review your strategy for the competition, check your equipment, and make the final adjustments to your focus and intensity. When the competition begins, you can perform to your fullest ability and ensure that you will be competitive from the very start.

Prime process. Another place in which athletes often see a decline in their performances is in the middle of a competition. It often occurs, for example, after halftime of a football or basketball game, at the beginning of the second set of a tennis match, or at the start of the back nine in golf. This decrease in performance is usually in response to being ahead or behind at that point in the competition. It is caused by a change in focus and intensity from earlier in the competition.

It is common after leading in a competition to experience a change in focus and a letdown in intensity. Being ahead in a competition can cause overconfidence and the belief that athletes will win the competition. When this thought, "I have it won," occurs, it signals to the mind and body that they can relax. Focus shifts away from what enabled athletes to gain the lead and their intensity drops so they're no longer physically capable of performing at that winning level. It can also cause athletes to change their strategy, "If I just play it safe now, I will win." Taylor's Law of Stupidity applies here: if it's working, change it. That is just dumb. If you have something that's working, you should stick with it.

After falling behind, there can be the tendency to become discouraged and lose confidence. If athletes think, "I can't win now," their focus shifts onto the negative thoughts and feelings and their intensity either drops because they give up or it goes up because it is very threatening for them to think that they will lose.

At the same time, Taylor's Law of Insanity often applies: doing the same thing and expecting different results. Many athletes don't consider whether they need to change their tactics at this point in the competition. Certainly, in some cases, if athletes stick with their game plan, it can come around and it can turn the competition in their favor. More often than not, though, athletes fall behind because their strategy is not working.

At this stage of the competition, several things need to be done to achieve prime process. First, you have to consider what you need to do tactically to maintain (if you're winning) or raise (if you're losing) your level of performance. It may be that you should just keep doing what you are doing or you need to figure out what you can do to turn the competition around. Then, you have to take active steps to reestablish prime focus. This usually involves returning to a process focus in which you focus on what you need to do to perform well. Finally, you need to use psych-up or psych-down techniques to reach your prime intensity.

Prime finish. This final step in a Prime Competition involves performing your best to the end of the competition, win or lose. An exciting and difficult thing about many sports such as baseball and tennis is that there is no clock to end the game. In these and other sports, the competition isn't over until someone wins the final point. Even in sports with time limits, athletes and teams have come back from seemingly impossible deficits and won with time running out. What this means is that, no matter how far you are behind, you're never completely out of it and the competition isn't lost until either your opponent wins the last point or the time runs out. Of course, this also means that, no matter how far ahead you are, your opponent is never out of it either.

As with prime start and prime process, your ability to have a prime finish is determined by your focus and your intensity. The hardest part of a competition is closing it out. It's common for athletes, when they have the opportunity to end the competition, to either become very nervous because they can't believe they're actually going to win, or experience a total letdown in their intensity because they've already mentally won the competition. Both of these occurrences are caused by the same thing: a shift from a process focus to an outcome focus. Which response you have will depend on your confidence in your ability and your experience with winning.

As soon as you start focusing on winning the competition, several possible scenarios may occur. By realizing that you can win, many thoughts and emotions are triggered about winning. Perhaps you have not won that much, so you really can't believe that you might win the competition. Or deep down you aren't sure you deserve to win. These thoughts will usually provoke doubt and anxiety which will, in turn, cause you to become cautious and tentative. When this happens, you have a shift from "I can win" to "I hope my opponent loses for me." You no longer have control of the competition or over whether you will win or lose it. Your only hope is that your opponent has already lost mentally and doesn't put up a fight.

If you have confidence in your ability and you have won regularly before, other thoughts and emotions may arise. The most common is: "I have this won." In a sense, you are mentally leaving the competition and picking up your trophy. There is just one minor problem; the competition isn't over yet and you haven't won. You are no longer focusing on those things that enabled you to get to this point in the competition where you can win. The prime intensity that allowed you to be in a position to win is no longer present, so you are physically incapable of maintaining your level of performance.

The solution for both of the scenarios is simple: maintain your process focus and your prime intensity. If you have been in this situation before, you can almost be assured that one of these two responses will occur. You can plan for them and be prepared to take the necessary steps to combat these changes when they arise.

If you're losing the competition, your greatest challenge is to not give up and to keep fighting. Knowing that your opponent is probably going to experience one of the above reactions should give you hope that you're not out of the competition. Most athletes you compete against will see their performances decline toward the end for these reasons. With this knowledge, you should gain renewed motivation to stay in the competition and increased confidence that you still have a chance.

With this reinvigoration, your goal is to stay with a process focus, move closer to your prime intensity, and figure out if you need to make any tactical changes to take advantage of this opportunity. Understand that these efforts will not guarantee that you will come back and win. Your opponent may simply be too tough or you might not have the ability to win this time. However, your efforts will certainly raise your game, enable you to put up a good fight to the end so your opponent has to earn the victory, and ensure that you have a prime finish.

> *"Consistency under pressure is a certain kind of psychological steadiness that I first noticed."*
>
> **Bill Russell**

CHAPTER ELEVEN

LESSONS FROM THE WORLD'S BEST

Prime Time is what competing in sports is all about. It's the reason why you work so hard on all aspects of your sport. Prime Time is the reason you're reading this book. The goal of *Prime Sport* is for you to perform your best in Prime Time. Prime Time refers to competitive situations that really matter. The situations that can turn a competition toward you or against you.

Prime Time is that moment that defines you as an athlete. It shows you and others how skilled you are, how well conditioned you are, and, most importantly, how strong you are mentally. This book has been directed toward you achieving Prime Sport and being able to use it in Prime Time.

This notion of Prime Time emerged from my work with one young athlete who was making a difficult, though successful, transition from high-level junior competition to the professional ranks. What became clear to both of us was that the professional level holds little resemblance to the juniors. The pros don't just do things better, they do things differently. These lessons that we learned together helped this athlete overcome the challenges of professional sport and attain a high world ranking. They also showed me things that athletes at all levels could use to raise their performances and achieve their highest level of competitive success. These lessons are divided into two categories: competitive and mental.

COMPETITIVE LESSONS

1. *Perform to the best of your ability.* At any given competition, you may not be at your best. You may not be performing that well due to fatigue, illness, injury, or any number of reasons. Whatever ability you bring to the competition, perform to the best of that ability. An important lesson I learned from working with world-class and professional athletes is that you can't always perform at 100%. Imagine the life of a high-level athlete. They travel and compete constantly, sometimes going from one side of the world to the other and having to compete the next day. There is simply no way they can be totally on top of their game for every competition.

Many times, athletes begin a competition and just don't feel very good, and know they're not going to perform well. Because they're not going to perform at 100%, they, in essence, throw in the towel before the competition even begins. They think, "If I'm not feeling good, there's no way I can perform well and win. So why even try."

However, as I said previously, you don't have to perform your best to win. You only need to perform better than your opponent. So, to increase the likelihood of that happening, you must learn to perform your best with what you have on that given day. For example, if you're only at 80%, perform at the full 80%. That may still be enough for you to win.

2. *KISS.* Most sports are quite simple. Whoever performs their best wins the competition. Yet, athletes can make sports complicated by trying to do too many things. A rule to follow is the KISS principle. Most athletes know the KISS principle as "keep it simple stupid," but I don't believe that one. I believe athletes should "keep it simple SMART!"

My KISS principle means that you should choose a few basic things you want to do in a competition and stick to them. When things aren't going well, there can be a tendency to think too much and try to find some complex solution to the problem. This approach usually just clouds the situation and makes it worse.

Your goal should be to focus on a few things and do them to the best of your ability. If you look at the top athletes, most don't make their sport complicated. Every great athlete does a few things well and has one or two strengths on which they rely. Pedro Martinez has his fastball. Martina Hingis has her tactics and footwork. Jaromir Jagr has his stick handling.

3.   *Have a plan.* Competing without a plan is like an army going to battle without a strategy to defeat the enemy. Firepower, that is to say ability, is not always enough to overcome an opponent. A well-conceived plan and superior tactics can often overcome a more skilled athlete. You have two goals in devising a game plan: maximize your strengths and exploit your opponent's weaknesses.

Before a competition, decide on a few basic tactics that you do well and that you will use. The most important contributor should be what are your strengths. It would make little sense to design a plan that you're not physically or technically capable of executing. A plan should emphasize your strengths and minimize your weaknesses.

The second thing to consider in developing a plan is your opponent's strengths and weaknesses. This input should be secondary to your capabilities because you wouldn't want to create a plan based on your opponent's weaknesses that you don't have the ability to execute. You may also not know anything about how your opponent performs. An ideal plan is one that utilizes your strengths and neutralizes your opponent's strengths. This strategy provides the opportunity to gain control of the competition by emphasizing what you do best and they do worst.

You also want to devise a backup plan in case Plan A doesn't work. If you recall my law of insanity, doing the same thing and expecting different results, you have to recognize when a plan isn't working and isn't going to work. Yet, it's difficult to come up with another plan in the heat of a competition. I recommend that you have a Plan B prepared before the competition. Plan B should have the same goals as Plan A of maximizing your strengths and neutralizing your opponent's weaknesses, but offer another way to accomplish the goal.

Having a Plan A and a Plan B provides several benefits. Foremost, you have a "method to your madness" during a competition. You're not just going out there and hoping to perform well and win. Rather, you have a plan designed to enable you to perform your best and maximize your chances of winning that will guide you through the competition. Having a game plan will also boost your confidence because you have a way that you believe will allow you to perform your best and win.

4.   *Expect it to be hard.* This is one of the toughest lessons for young athletes who are making the transition from the juniors to the world-class and professional ranks. As juniors, there are always easy competitions. Because they are at such a high level, they will often be competing against athletes who have much less ability. Not at the professional level. Every competition is hard. Every competition is one they could lose because their opponents are just as good, just as competitive, and just as hungry to win.

Athletic competition should be difficult. That is what makes it so much fun and rewarding. If you perform against someone whom you are considerably better than and you win, how do you feel? Not much sense of accomplishment and satisfaction, is there? Competition is supposed to be hard. It should be physically demanding. Competitions should test your technical and tactical capabilities. It should show you what you are made of mentally and emotionally. That is why you compete. This is even more true when you perform in Prime Time.

If you expect it to be hard, then there will be no surprises. If you fall behind, well, that is part of sports. If you choke, well, that happens. If you fight as hard as you can and still lose, well, you can still feel good for having given your best effort. If you expect it to be hard, you will prepare yourself physically and mentally for the demands of competition. When the competition proves that you were right, it is tough, then you'll respond well and perform your best.

5. *Win the mental game.* As I alluded to in the preface, when you begin a competition, you compete in two games. First, you compete against your opponent in the actual competition. Second, you compete against yourself in the mental game. Your opponent has a similar situation. Given fairly equal ability, whoever wins the mental game will win the competition.

There are several keys to winning the mental game. Most importantly, you have to be your best ally rather than your worst enemy. If your opponent is against you and you are against you, you don't have a chance. Another key is to never give up. Remember what happens when you give up; you automatically lose. As long as you stay motivated and keep fighting no matter how you're performing, you will always have a chance. Two essential mental skills are to maintain prime focus and intensity throughout the competition. Without these two Prime Sport skills, you will not be physically or mentally capable of performing your best. This entire book is designed to help you win the mental game.

> *"The simplest definition of a champion is the one with self-awareness closest to reality and seems able to execute best under pressure."*
>
> **Billie Jean King**

MENTAL LESSONS

1. *Believe in your ability.* As Chapter Three suggests, developing confidence in your ability is one of the biggest challenges you face. Except for the very best in the world, many athletes don't have that deeply ingrained belief in their capabilities. I see this often early in a competition. For example, a figure skater misses a jump early in the free program and proceeds to take out other difficult jumps because he has lost confidence in himself, even though there is ample evidence from his training and past competitions that he is highly capable of executing the difficult jumps.

This confidence in their ability is an essential quality that separates the great athletes from the good ones. Through experience and success, they gain such trust in their capabilities that even when they are not performing well, they keep going for it. They have such confidence that they know that if they just keep trying and not allow themselves to become tentative, their performance will improve.

It's a mistake for the figure skater in the last example to change his program just because it doesn't work right away. Instead, this athlete should stick to his program. A lesson you can take from the world's best athletes is to believe in your ability and know that it will, in time, enable you to perform your best.

This belief will also serve athletes well in Prime Time. Imagine a soccer player who has successfully kicked thousands of penalty kicks in practice and games. Yet, the essential question is, Can she make a penalty kick in the shootout of the most important game of her life, like Brandi Chastain did in the 1999 Women's World Cup final? A lesson you can learn from the best athletes in the world is to develop such a belief in your ability that you truly know that you can perform your best when you absolutely need to. This belief in your ability gives you the confidence to go for it in Prime Time.

2.   *Be ready for every performance.* One of the first lessons young professionals learn when they make to the major leagues, the NBA, NFL, ATP, or LPGA is that there are no easy wins. Every performance is an opportunity to perform well or poorly. The type of performance that is had depends largely on how prepared athletes are to perform.

This is important for young professionals and their opponents. Young professionals can expect that their more experienced opponents will make them work every step of the way. They must also be sure not to give easy wins away. Loose performances at critical stages of a competition can mean the difference between who wins and who loses.

A lesson you can learn from the pros is to take your time and be sure that you are physically, technically, tactically, and mentally ready for every performance. This practice serves several purposes. It enables you to recover physically and mentally from the last performance. You can focus on the present and the process which will enable you to be more prepared for the next performance. It also enables you to reduce your intensity which can be expected to rise, especially if the next performance is an important one. By taking extra time, you can also develop a plan of how you want to perform.

Most importantly, your goal is to ensure that when you begin the next performance, you are totally prepared to perform your best. Only by being completely ready for every performance will you be able to perform well consistently and achieve Prime Sport.

3.   *Expect to be nervous in Prime Time.* Prime Time means the competition matters. It may be the finals of a big tournament or you may be in overtime. You may start to feel nervous because the competition is on the line. This anxiety makes you uncomfortable, which raises doubts in your mind, causes you to feel negative emotions, and, because of all of these, you become more nervous. As a result, the quality of your performance declines and you lose the competition.

This reaction is common among athletes of all levels of ability. It is also one of the most harmful to Prime Sport. Much of this book is directed toward helping you achieve prime intensity and not experience anxiety under pressure. The reality is, though, getting nervous before and during important competitions is normal and natural. It happens to club athletes and it happens to the best athletes in the world.

One way to partially alleviate the negative effects of this nervousness is to expect be to nervous in Prime Time. If you anticipate experiencing some anxiety, when it arises, your reaction will be, "This is normal. I knew I would get a little nervous. No big deal," instead of "Oh no. I can't believe I'm getting nervous now. How can I perform well feeling this way?"

Anxiety can also be interpreted in different ways producing very different reactions. If you view anxiety as negative and threatening, it will clearly hurt your performance. If you see it, instead, as an indication that you're getting yourself prepared for an important competition or a key performance, then the feeling will be interpreted as getting psyched up rather than as getting nervous, and you will see it much more positively. With a more positive perspective on the added intensity, it will be less likely to produce negative thoughts and emotions, and, as a result, it will have a less harmful effect on your performance.

Another important realization is that whatever you're feeling, your opponent is probably feeling the same doubts, anxiety, and emotions. Even if they look cool, calm, and collected on the outside, the chances are they're equally as nervous on the inside. This perspective offers even more support for the need to win the mental game. Given fairly equal ability, the athlete who wins the mental game is most likely going to win the competition.

4. *Recover from mistakes quickly.* If you recall, Prime Sport is based on the notion that you can perform at a consistently high level under challenging conditions. However, performing consistently does not mean that you will not make mistakes or experience declines in your level of performance. One of the things that makes the world's best athletes so good is not that they don't make mistakes, but rather how quickly they recover from them. Competitions are often won or lost based on which athlete can recover from their mistakes most quickly.

It's not uncommon for athletes to take a long time to recover from a mistake at a key point in a competition. This occurs because they lose confidence, focus, and intensity, and they become frustrated, angry, or depressed due to their mistakes. It can take a while for them to get their head and their performance together again and get back into the competition. Unfortunately, by the time they recover mentally and raise their level of performance to its previous level, the competition may be lost.

Recovering from mistakes quickly begins with a forgiving attitude in which you accept that you will make mistakes and you understand that negative thoughts and emotions, and poor focus and intensity will cause you to perform worse. Accepting mistakes as part of sports will make it easier for you to let go of the mistakes.

With the negative impact of mistakes reduced, you can then direct your attention to getting yourself back mentally and emotionally. This process begins with maintaining your confidence with positive thinking and body language. You can then redirect your focus onto the process and the present, in other words, what you need to do to improve your performance. You can also check and adjust your intensity to ensure your body is prepared to perform at its prime level.

Having dealt with the mental and emotional aspects of mistakes, you can then directly address the cause of your poor performance. You want to recognize that you have a problem as soon as possible. If a pattern starts to emerge in which you make the same mistake repeatedly, you should recognize that you have a problem that needs to be addressed. You can then identify the problem and find a solution. The problem might be technical or tactical. To solve the problem, you will need to make an adjustment in your performance and focus on the solution in the immediate future.

5.   *Accept the challenge.* The biggest obstacle to Prime Sport is fear. Fear produces in athletes a cautious attitude and a tentative approach to performance. On a practical level, this means that your main goal is to just play it safe and hope not to make too big a mistake. You don't perform aggressively, take risks, or push yourself to your highest level of performance.

There are few things more unsatisfying than going down with a whimper, not a bang. Athletes usually feel terrible when they perform scared and they always regret having performed so tentatively. This style of performance simply won't work because for every performance in fear, their opponent may be performing with excitement.

Accepting the challenge does not mean performing on the edge every moment of a competition. It means that whatever you are doing in a competition, you give it everything you have. It means putting all of your focus, intensity, and energy into performing your very best.

Before a competition, accept the challenge to perform with courage and the willingness to risk in order to achieve Prime Sport. Resolve to perform to your fullest ability. Commit to doing everything you can to perform your best and win the competition. Accept that when you have this attitude, you still may not win. Understand that in Prime Time you can't always control whether you win or lose, but you can control the effort you put in, how hard you fight, and how well you perform. If you do that, then you're much more likely to achieve Prime Sport and, win or lose, you will feel good about how you performed.

> *"I was fearing the challenge instead of embracing it. There's a subtle but important difference there. I want to feel I'm licking my chops all the time at life. And that's the way I want to approach running."*
>
> **World-class runner Melody Fairchild**

SECTION V:

PRIME SPORT PLAN

CHAPTER TWELVE

PRIME SPORT GOAL SETTING

Goal setting is essential to being the best athlete you can be. Motivation is not enough to be your best. Motivation without goals is like knowing where you want to go without knowing how to get there. Goals act as the road map to your desired destination. Goals increase your commitment and motivation and provide deliberate steps toward your competitive aspirations.

A Prime Sport goal-setting program begins with a vision of where you want to go and what you want to do in your sport. It also provides a clear why, what, where, and how for your efforts in striving for Prime Sport. The Prime Sport Goal Formula (see below) illustrates the important role that goals perform in becoming a better athlete.

PRIME TENNIS GOAL FORMULA

Motivation + Goals = PROGRESS

TYPES OF GOALS

There are five types of goals that you want to set in your Prime Sport goal-setting program. *Long-term* goals represent what you ultimately want to achieve in your sport such as to win the club championship, receive a college scholarship, or compete at the professional level. *Yearly* goals indicate what you want to achieve in the next 12 months, for example, to attain a certain ranking or qualify for a particular competition. *Competitive* goals specify how you want to perform in competitions you'll be in during the coming year. *Training* goals represent what you need to do in your physical, technical, tactical, and mental training to achieve your competitive goals. *Lifestyle* goals indicate what you need to do in your general lifestyle to reach your goals such as sleep, diet, work or school, and relationships.

Lower goals should support and lead progressively to the higher goals. For example, your lifestyle goals should help you accomplish your training goals which, in turn, should lead to your competitive goals, which should enable you to reach your yearly goals which finally should allow you to achieve your long-term goals.

> *"Unless you're really dedicated to a goal, there's no point in doing it."*
>
> **World skiing gold medallist Hilary Lindh**

GOAL GUIDELINES

The effectiveness of a Prime Sport goal-setting program depends on whether you understand what kinds of goals to set and how to use them to enhance your motivation and direction. There are six goal guidelines you should follow to get the most out of your goal setting.

1.   *Goals should be challenging, but realistic and attainable.* You should set goals that can be reached, but only with time and effort. If you set

goals that are too easy, you'll reach them with little effort, so they will do little for your motivation. If you set goals that are too difficult, you won't be able to achieve them no matter how hard you try. This wouldn't help your motivation either since there would be little point in putting out effort toward a goal you know you can't reach.

2.   *Goals should be specific and concrete.* It's not sufficient to set a goal such as "I want to improve my strength this year." Goals should be clearly stated and measurable. For example, "I want to increase my strength by 10% in three months." This goal indicates the precise area to be worked on, the specific amount of improvement aimed for, and the time frame in which to achieve the goal.

3.   *Focus on degree of, rather than absolute, goal attainment.* An inevitable part of goal setting is that you won't reach all of your goals because it's not possible to accurately judge what is realistic for all goals. If you're only concerned with whether you reach a goal, you may see yourself as a failure if you're unable to do so. This response will invariably reduce rather than bolster your motivation. You should be more concerned with how much of the goal you achieve (degree of attainment) rather than whether or not you fully reach the goal (absolute attainment). Though you won't attain all of your goals, you will almost always improve toward a goal. With this perspective, if you don't reach a goal, but still improve 50% over the previous level, you're more likely to view yourself as having been successful in achieving the goal.

4.   *Goal setting is a dynamic and fluid process.* Goal setting is a process that never ends. When one goal is achieved, you should set another goal that is higher or in a different direction to continually allow yourself to improve. You should review your goals regularly, compare them to actual progress, and adjust them as needed. Because you won't be able to set goals with perfect accuracy, you must be open to making changes as needed. For example, goals that you reach more easily than expected should be immediately reset to a higher level. Conversely, if you set goals that were too difficult to achieve, you should modify them to a more realistic level.

5. *Prepare a written contract.* Research suggests that goal setting is most effective when it's prepared as a written contract comprised of explicit statements of your goals and the specific way you will achieve them. This approach clearly identifies your goals and holds you accountable for the fulfillment of the contract. You can complete a goal-setting contract, sign it, and give copies to your coach and others. To ensure that you continue to follow the contract, you can meet periodically with your coach to review your goals.

6. *Get regular feedback.* One of the most important contributors to the effectiveness of a Prime Sport goal-setting program is consistent feedback. You should get regular feedback about how you're doing in pursuing your goals. This information can come from coaches, video analysis, physical testing, or with Prime Sport Profiling. Consistent feedback that you're reaching your goals reinforces your motivation by showing you that your efforts are resulting in progress.

Using the Prime Sport Goal Setting form (see page 167), write down your goals following the goal guidelines I just described. If you're uncertain of what your goals should be, ask your coach, your trainer, or others who know what you're working on.

> *"The resources of the human body and soul are enormous and beyond our present knowledge and expectations. We go part of the way to consciously tapping these resources by having goals that we want desperately."*
>
> **Olympic track & field champion Herb Elliot**

PRIME SPORT GOAL SETTING

Directions: I n the space below, indicate your Long-term, Yearly, and Competitive goals.

Long-Term (ultimate sport dream):

Yearly (performance and ranking goals for the year):

Competitive (goals for specific competitions):

PRIME SPORT GOAL SETTING (cont.)

Directions: In the space below, set your Training and Lifestyle goals that will enable you to achieve your Competitive, Yearly, and Long -term goals. Also, under Method, indicate specifically how you will reach your Training and Lifestyle goals. Examples have been provided in *italics* for each type of goal.

Training (goals for all aspects of preparation):

Technical (*biomechanics, tactics*)

    1.
        Method:

    2.
        Method:

    3.
        Method:

Physical (*strength, stamina, agility*)

    1.
        Method:

    2.
        Method:

    3.
        Method:

PRIME SPORT GOAL SETTING (cont.)

Mental (*motivation, confidence, intensity, focus, emotions*)

    1.
       Method:

    2.
       Method:

    3.
       Method:

Lifestyle (sleep, diet, work/school, relationships):

    1.
       Method:

    2.
       Method:

    3.
       Method:

CHAPTER THIRTEEN

PRIME SPORT PROGRAM

You now know what your goals are. The aim of the Prime Sport program is to help you achieve these goals in the most efficient and organized way possible. You can develop your own individualized Prime Sport program by following three steps: design, implementation, and maintenance.

DESIGN

The first thing you must do in the *design* phase of developing your Prime Sport program is to identify your most crucial mental needs. You can use the results from your Prime Sport profile to help you specify what mental areas you need to work on most. You'll also have different areas you need to work on in different sport settings. For example, focus might be most important when you're training, developing your sport imagery skills may be most necessary off-sport, and controlling your intensity may be most critical when you're competing. Using the Prime Sport Identification form (see page 172), list the mental areas that you want to focus on in training, off-sport, and in competitions.

The next thing you need to do in designing your Prime Sport program is to specify Prime Sport techniques you will use to develop the mental

170

areas you've just identified. It's not feasible to use every Prime Sport technique for a certain area. For example, I described six strategies you could use to build your confidence. You should narrow those choices to two or three techniques that you like most. To do this, experiment with the different techniques for a few days and see which ones you're most comfortable with. Once again using the Prime Sport Identification form, list the two or three techniques you've chosen. I recommend that sport imagery be a regular part of your off-sport Prime Sport program because it offers so many benefits to every mental area.

The final part of the design phase is to organize your Prime Sport program into a daily and weekly schedule. Just as you plan your physical and technical training, you want to specify when you will be doing your Prime Sport training. The Typical Prime Sport Program (see page 173) illustrates how you can organize Prime Sport techniques into a cohesive program. Using the Prime Sport Planner (see page 175), indicate when and where you will use Prime Sport techniques you've specified in the Prime Sport Identification form.

> *"We need to know where we are going, and how we plan to get there. Our dreams and aspirations must be translated into real and tangible goals, with priorities and a time frame. All of these should be in writing, so that it can be reviewed, updated, and revised as necessary."*

Former NFL great Merlin Olsen

PRIME SPORT IDENTIFICATION

Directions: In the space below, indicate the mental areas on which you n eed to work in   the different settings. Then, specify Prime Sport techniques you will use to develop these areas.

Setting	Mental Area	Prime Sport Techniques
Training		
1.		
2.		
3.		
Off-Sport		
1.		
2.		
3.		
Competitions		
1.		
2.		
3.		

TYPICAL PRIME SPORT PROGRAM

Mental Need and Goal	Mental Technique	Place in Schedule
Increase Motivation	Goal setting	Before season; monthly
	Two daily questions	At start and end of day
Build Confidence	Athlete's Litany training	At start and end of
	Thought-stopping	In training and and competitions
Intensity Control	Deep breathing	During training and competitions
	Active relaxation	At end of training
	Sport routines	Before competitions; between performances
Overall Performance	Sport imagery	Three times per week before dinner

IMPLEMENTATION

The second phase of the Prime Sport program is *implementation*. This is where you put into action the Prime Sport program you've just designed. It's best that you begin your Prime Sport program as far in advance of your primary competitive season as possible. There are several benefits to starting your Prime Sport program early. It enables you to develop the most effective Prime Sport program possible. An early start allows you to incorporate it fully into your overall training program. It lets you fine-tune the program to best suit your needs. Most importantly, it gives you the time to practice the skills and gain its benefits.

A concern that athletes often have is the time commitment required for a Prime Sport program. Certainly, they are busy enough without introducing one more thing into their lives, no matter how important it is. Athletes can spend hours every day in their physical and technical training and there simply wouldn't be similar time to devote to their Prime Sport program. Fortunately, Prime Sport training doesn't require hours a day to gain its benefits. Most Prime Sport training can be incorporated directly into a traditional sport training program. Only about 10-15 minutes a day extra is needed for outside Prime Sport training such as relaxation and sport imagery.

If you feel that all of the areas and techniques you've identified in your Prime Sport program are too much to do, then start small. Select half the techniques you've specified and work on those. You'll find that Prime Sport training is not only not time consuming or overwhelming, but rather it is an enjoyable addition to your current training program and a nice break from your usual routine. You'll also find that you pick up Prime Sport techniques quickly and you'll get to the point where you do them without thinking about it.

> *"Tara [Lipinski] has her day structured so she's a giddy teenager between these hours and a really hard worker between these hours."*
>
> **Coach Richard Callaghan**

PRIME SPORT PLANNER

Time	Monday	Tuesday	Wednesday	Thursday	Friday	Saturday	Sunday
MORNING							
AFTERNOON							
EVENING							

MAINTENANCE

The final phase of the Prime Sport program is *maintenance*. The reality is that there is no end to the use of Prime Sport training. Just like physical conditioning and technical skills, mental skills will atrophy when they're not maintained through regular use. As I described in the Positive Change Formula, repetition is essential for you to maintain Prime Sport. Fortunately, with practice, Prime Sport skills become automatic, so you need less time and effort to retain them. For example, once you've developed your focus skills, it's easier to stay focused, so you don't have to pay as much attention to your focusing techniques.

Once you achieve Prime Sport, you can adjust your Prime Sport program to a lower, though still consistent, level of involvement. Also, as new problems arise, you can modify your Prime Sport program to resolve them.

POSTSCRIPT

To be motivated, confident, intense, and focused. To be an emotional master. To be your best ally rather than your worst enemy. To perform your best consistently under the most challenging conditions. These are the skills that Prime Sport can help you develop.

Why is Prime Sport so important to you that you would read this book and put such time and effort into your sport? Your answer is a personal one. For some, it may be to have more fun in their sport. For others, it may be to become the best athlete they possibly can. For still others, it may be to win more.

I would like to believe, though, that the most compelling reason why you want to achieve Prime Sport is to master what I have described as the most important and difficult game in which you compete, in your sport and in your life. That game is the *mental game*. If you can win the mental game and remove all of the obstacles that keep you from performing your best and living your fullest life, then everything is possible.

By winning the mental game, you clear the path to happiness, fulfillment, and success in sports and, yes, in life. I hope that, as you have read *Prime Sport*, you've thought, "Hey, this could apply to my work" or "This relates to my relationships." Sport, like life, is filled with challenges, struggles, excitement, setbacks, failures, and ultimately, mastery. Because to experience the "triumph of the athlete mind" is also to seize victory in the game of life.

Jim Taylor, Ph.D.
October, 2000

REFERENCES

Apter, M. J. (1989). *Reversal theory: Motivation, emotion, and personality.* London: Routledge.

Butler, R. J., & Hardy, L. (1992). The performance profile: Theory and application. *The Sport Psychologist,* **6**, 253-264.

Cautela, J. R., & Wisocki, P. A. (1977). Thought-stoppage procedure: Description, application, and learning theory applications. *Psychological Records,* **27**, 255-264.

Ericsson, K., & Charnes, N. (1994). Expert performance: Its structure and acquisition. *American Psychologist,* **49**, 725-747.

Jacobson, E. (1930). *Progressive relaxation.* Chicago: University of Chicago.

Moran, A. (1996). *The psychology of concentration in sport performers: A cognitive analysis.* East Sussex, UK: Psychology.

Nideffer, R. M. (1981). *The ethics and practice of applied sport psychology.* Ithaca, NY: Mouvement.

Singer, R. N., Murphey, M., & Tennant, L. K. (Eds.). (1993). *Handbook of research on sport psychology.* New York: MacMillan.

Taylor, J. (1996). *The mental edge for sports* (4th ed.). Denver, CO: Minuteman.

Van Raalte, J. L., & Brewer, B. W. (Eds.). (1996). *Exploring sport and exercise psychology.* Washington, DC: APA.

Williams, J. M. (Ed.). (1998). *Applied sport psychology: Personal growth to peak performance* (3rd ed.) (pp. 219-236). Palo Alto, CA Mayfield.

ABOUT THE AUTHOR

Dr. Jim Taylor has been a consultant to the U.S. and Japanese Ski Teams, and the U.S. Tennis Association. He has worked with junior-elite, collegiate, world-class, and professional athletes in tennis, skiing, golf, football, baseball, hockey, track & field, cycling, swimming, volleyball, water skiing, and other sports. His clients include athletes from the NFL, NBA, MLB, PGA, ATP, and WTA. Dr. Taylor received his bachelor's degree from Middlebury College and earned his M.A. and Ph.D. in Psychology from the University of Colorado. He is a former associate professor and Director of Sport Psychology at Nova University in Ft. Lauderdale. A former alpine ski racer who held a top-20 national ranking and competed internationally, Dr. Taylor is a United States Professional Tennis Association certified teaching professional, a 2nd degree black belt and certified instructor in karate, and a marathon runner. He is also the author of thirteen books including the *Prime Sport book series* and *Psychological Approaches to Sports Injury Rehabilitation*. Dr. Taylor has published over 220 articles in popular and professional publications and has given more than 300 workshops and presentations throughout the United States, Canada, and Europe.